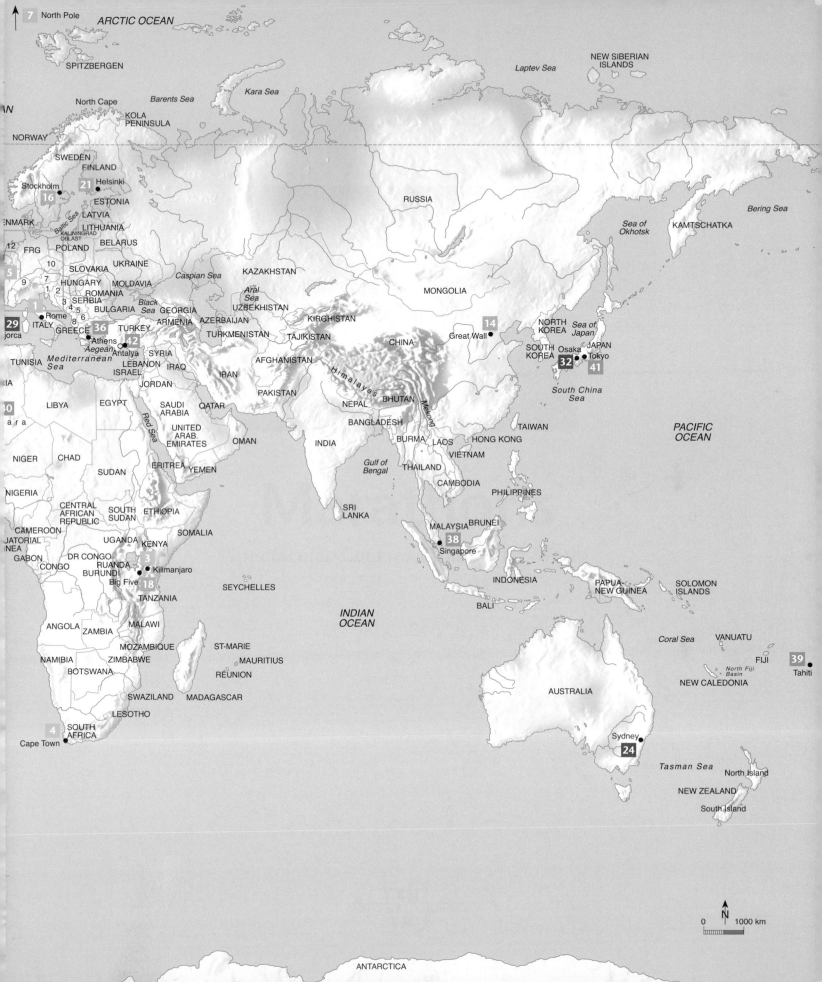

Marathons

Spectacular Courses Around the World

Urs Weber

Contents

A marathon puts everyone in a good mood: the runners (top, in Majorca) as they run through beautiful cities or beneath palm trees in Tahiti (center), and also the spectators and helpers such as these ones at the New York Marathon (bottom).

All marathon runners are winners when it comes to the finish line, whether in Venice or in Vienna (center, top/bottom)

There are marathon journeys to all kinds of destinations. And so runners discover the world, meet similarly minded people and enjoy unique experiences in nature.

The marathon dream

So you too are thinking of taking part in a marathon? Or you are looking for a completely different marathon destination? Then this is the right book for you. Because in it you will discover the incredible fascination of marathon running. It will even enthral those of you who have never run a marathon and who perhaps may never run one.

Marathon running involves great willpower, a sporting ambition and above average physical fitness, but also requires determined curiosity to discover yourself and the world around you.

This book gives 42 reasons for the fascination for marathons: 42 marathon events that promise a very special running experience and that will also offer even more than running—a long-lasting memory. One does not run a marathon every weekend. Many runners run just one marathon in their life. And because it is such a fantastic event for you, it is important to choose an equally fantastic location.

You can start in front of you own front door or at the other end of the world. A marathon run is a two-dimensional experience. First of all, it is always exciting—even after the first marathon—to see how we react to the challenge, how one experiences the marathon and how one survives it: the nerves before the start, the strength during the first few miles, then the exhaustion setting in, the mental and physical struggle with oneself—and the subsequent recuperation. The other dimension is experiencing the place itself where you are running this 26.2-mile (42.195 km) race. Marathon runners are very much aware of their surroundings which they greatly appreciate. There are also many meetings that occur automatically with other runners and the local people. The marathons selected for this book work in both dimensions. If you run in a beautiful place you will also have a very special personal experience.

Marathon journeys round the world
When running a marathon you naturally form a close bond with the place in which you are running. That is why a marathon journey is very much worth while. For instance, the New York Marathon is a fantastic discovery tour of this unique city while a South Seas marathon will bring you closer to nature, as will running the marathon distance at the North Pole.

These running events taking place in the most diverse regions of the world and the ones described here will help you decide which region, which city and which climate appeals to you. The selection made for this book is quite subjective and follows no strict requirements or specification, but it aims to show the great range

of marathons and the different kinds of experience that the marathon adventure can offer you.

Perhaps you will also discover a completely new motivation, a secret longing or a new ambition. When choosing exactly you want to run, you will find that there are many convincing reasons for your choice. But if running is your hobby, you can go entirely by your instinct.

Equally, people may ask you why you actually want to run a marathon. Ironically, people who are enthusiastic runners themselves will not ask you such a question. And someone who is not a runner will probably not understand your reasons.

In fact there are thousands of good reasons to run a marathon. It is not illogical as some people might think but rather it is a remarkable ambition. This aspect becomes very obvious in the descriptions of the various marathon destinations. When you return from one of these marathons, your life will have been immeasurably enriched.

Whether you only concentrate on yourself and you best possible performance or on the route and its surroundings: the experience is always very intense.

11

Spring

Spring is also "the time of awakening" for marathon runners. The changes in the air and the surrounding are noticeable as soon as you start running. Each day, the sun rises a little earlier and the temperature becomes a little warmer. Nature is becoming fragrant again. Now the training carried out during the winter months is bearing fruit. The harvest will follow in the first spring marathon.

Off at last: The Two Oceans Marathon is a highlight of the spring

Rome is the setting of one of the year's first opportunities to compete in a big-city marathon. Held in the spring, the pleasant weather is warm enough to wear shorts. An additional attraction is the spectacular backdrop of the ancient city.

Rome Marathon

With the blessing of the Pope

In the city where history lies in almost every stone, Rome's Marathon also has an impressive history. The event is superbly orchestrated and the historic setting has a tremendous impact on the Rome Marathon.

Few Olympic victories have been as memorable as that of Abebe Bikila in the 1960 Olympic Games in Rome. The Ethiopian wearing race number 11 set a world record (2:15:16). And he ran barefoot! It was the first Olympic medal won by an African athlete in the history of the Olympic Games. Today such a feat seems unremarkable in view of the supremacy of African runners in long-distance races, but at the time it was a real sensation. As European sports journalists wrote, he was an amateur, but he was extremely well trained. Photographs of this Marathon went all over the world: Bikila leading the race barefoot on tarmac, dusty roads or cobblestones, with sweat glistening on his dark skin. The marathon started in the late afternoon and ended at night. The Via Appia was lined with soldiers every 27 yards (25 m), each one holding a torch to illuminate the route. Bikila was then almost unknown in the world of sport, and in honor of his triumph the race number 11 is no longer issued. His victory was great publicity for the Marathon itself and for the city of Rome, since these were

the first Olympic Games in which the Marathon was broadcast in its entirety on television. It was also the first time that the whole route was reserved for runners alone and closed to cars. The organization was perfect. In addition to the television viewers, numerous spectators gathered along the route; the Marathon was a modern spectacle for the masses and it enjoyed a real boost in popularity.

Classical surroundings

Today the Rome Marathon is still one of the most spectacular events in Europe and it has its own characteristic atmosphere. As it has always done, it continues to win high marks for the quality of its organization. But it must be said that today there will be about 15,000 runners. This inevitably leads to long waits, bottlenecks and physical contact with other runners. The Rome Marathon is the biggest such event in Italy and it attracts many enthusiasts from outside that country, who make up 40 percent or more of those on the start line. Locals declare that it is the most beautiful

marathon in the world, and it is easy to understand this feeling. The race starts near the Colosseum where the runners congregate at the Arch of Constantine. A stage designer would revel in the scene with crowds of colorful marathon runners set off by the classical background. The Italian runners celebrate and sing loudly with the music which begins to play before the start of the race. The Via dei Fori Imperiali is a superb starting point for a marathon. Even before the start the runners feel elated at being here, so the pre-race tension moves up a notch.

A divine mission

The incomparable position of the Rome Marathon was carried to new heights in the year 2000, when the race started exceptionally on New Year's Day and in St. Peter's Square. Pope John Paul II blessed the runners before the start of the race. "On a divine mission:" here this description takes on a completely new dimension. True, the connection between religion and running is not a widely recognized concept in the world of marathon and everyday running, and biblical references associating running with Christianity are rare. But there is an example in St. Paul's First Epistle to the Corinthians, (9:24): "Do you not realize that, though all the runners in the stadium take part in the race, only one of them gets the prize? Run like that—to win."

The Victor Emmanuel monument in the Piazza Venezia (top), the Vatican City, the Colosseum, the Roman Forum and numerous other fine buildings. The Rome Marathon is hard to beat in terms of sights to be seen along the route.

Inspiration from the past. The last part of the route leads to the Colosseum and around it. The finish line is not far away up the Via dei Fori Imperiali, where each runner who finishes receives the coveted marathon medal.

There was another occasion when the Pope played an important part in the Rome Marathon, although in completely different way, and that was in 2013. Pope Benedict XVI, the first German Pope, felt he could no longer carry out his duties because of his age and health.

The Conclave was called in which 115 cardinals of the Roman Catholic Church would gather in the Sistine Chapel to elect a new Pope. The date was a highly charged one for the Marathon—only six days before the start. It was a tight situation, with tourists arriving for the papal election and the Marathon route being near the Vatican, so the organizers had already thought of an alternative route. But participants who had registered for the Marathon were concerned about the less attractive route, the complications of the journey and even that the event might be cancelled. In addition to the 14,000 or so marathon runners, there were also going to be about 80,000 participants in the Fun Run of 2.48 miles (4 km). Then on the Wednesday before the Sunday of the Marathon, white smoke was seen rising from the chimney of the Sistine Chapel against the blue sky: "Habemus papam—We have a pope." As a result some 150,000 of the faithful flocked to St. Peter's Square on the Sunday of the Marathon to attend the Angelus prayer of the new Pope, Francis.

It is likely that the clergy had little faith in the spiritual force of the run, and it is thought that representatives of the Vatican tried to have the Marathon cancelled. But in the end, the marathon organizers prevailed, agreeing as a compromise to make a small change in the route near St. Peter's Square and to delay the starting time a little.

Tourist high points

Runners who respond to the beauty of their surroundings and enjoy tourist sights will be thrilled from the very start of the Rome Marathon. The route starts by the Forum and the grandiose Piazza Venezia. Here the runners will see the sparkling white Victor Emmanuel II Monument, a striking demonstration that monumental art is always a matter of taste. Then follows the Capitoline Hill, steeped in history and originally the political and religious center of Rome. A little further on the ruins of the Circus Maximus can be seen on the right, the stadium 656 yards (600 m) long which hosted spectacular chariot races in ancient Rome. Over 150,000 spectators would come and watch the legendary chariot races which are still reconstructed today. The Marathon runners will reach the 3.1 miles (5 km) marker at Via Ostiense. Along the straight the front group of runners will slowly become more spread out. The more energetic runners will now be finding their rhythm. The route now runs along the Palatine, one of the seven hills of Rome and surely one of the places most steeped in history. According to the legend it was here that Romulus founded the city in 754 BC. Historically there is no doubt that it was the earliest populated site, and it was in this area that many Roman emperors built their residences and palaces.

Along the Tiber

The Tiber is crossed for the first time at 4.35 miles (7 km). Wide and usually muddy brown in color, the river is awe-inspiring while emanating a feeling of tranquility. It is the most constant companion in the Marathon as the runners follow its west bank into the center of Rome. Along the way they pass Tiber Island, the largest in the Tiber. One of the highlights comes soon after 9.32 miles (15 km) when the route crosses the Ponte Cavour and into the Via Crescenzio. On the left is the mighty Castle Sant'Angelo and a little further on the Vatican City becomes the focus of the runners' attention. In St. Peter's Square there is hardly a runner who does not cast a respectful glance towards St. Peter's Basilica and the Vatican City. After a northern loop, the second half of the race leads back to the center: the Piazza del Popolo, the Villa Borghese, the Spanish Steps and the Trevi Fountain are just a few of the tourist sights that are passed along the route

Barefoot across the finishing line

There is an interesting custom that is typically Roman and quite unique. After reaching the Colosseum, a few yards before the end of the marathon, some runners remove their shoes and cross the finishing line barefoot. This tradition has nothing to do with blisters on the feet or a religious ritual. It is rather a sporting acknowledgement to Abebe Bikila who ran the whole Marathon barefoot.

"First or last—all of us cross the same finish line."
Dean Karnazes

INFORMATION

DATE Second half of March
PARTICIPANTS About 15,000 starters

NATURE OF THE ROUTE This is a mostly flat city circuit that is defined by the historic sites of the city. The many stretches paved with cobblestones emphasize the historic nature of the Marathon, but they also require the runner to keep a watchful eye on the ground. It is also something to be remembered when choosing footwear; these stretches are not for people with wobbly knees or weak ankles. The event is very well organized. There are many casual runners at the start of the Marathon. Even more casual runners (up to 80,000) take part in the 2.48 mile (4 km) race.
ENTRY FEE About $70 (£40)
THE CITY Rome stands out among all the other European capitals. Few cities have such a rich history and this is clearly reflected in the large number of travel books devoted to the "Eternal City." Rome has an enormous number of historical, religious, cultural, and architectural sites and buildings.
TIP FOR RUNNERS Enjoy the unusual situation: all the streets on the Marathon route are completely closed to the traffic.
CONTACT DETAILS
Rome Marathon
Viale B. Bardanzellu, 65
00155 Rome
Italy
Tel.: +39 06 406 50 64
Fax: + 39 06 406 50 63
E-Mail: info@maratonadiroma.it

The start is at the Plaça Espanya (top), bathed in the early morning light. Later the route passes the celebrated Sagrada Familia by the Catalan architect Antoni Gaudí (bottom).

Barcelona Marathon

Past the sites of the fashionable capital

Hardly any city in Europe has developed as fast in the last decade as Barcelona. Its economic success has been accompanied by a flourishing fashion sector and cultural expansion, both regionally and internationally. The Marathon route takes in a large number of tourist attractions.

Barcelona in March is like New York or London in early May. Except of course for the palm trees on the sea front where the Spanish go for a stroll in their Sunday best: white shirt and polished shoes are part of the tradition. The dry, pleasantly warm air makes running very pleasant. But Barcelona is a very different place from New York, as is its Marathon. For the first few miles there is nothing much to note: the runners may see a few early-risers on their way to the baker, but spectators are few. Barcelona's streets are nearly empty except on the stretches where the route becomes very narrow. A long, gentle climb leads to the first place of interest on the route, FC Barcelona's Camp Nou Stadium, a concrete edifice which comes alive with the fans' enthusiasm for this top football club. But many runners will barely notice the stadium as they pass it. The next places of interest are Catalonia Boulevard, various Antoni

Gaudí buildings and the impressive Cathedral. The route through the Catalan capital is mainly level and passes by nearly all the tourist places of interest. The Marathon route also gives an idea of Barcelona's trendy side: several pop groups perform along the route and DJs play cool music, a pleasant diversion for the runners. By mid-morning it is really warm and the route makes a welcome loop to the promenade along the sea front. There the palm trees provide some shade and there is a pleasant cooling breeze.

The slower runners in sight
In Barcelona too the characteristics of a loop course must be accepted: on entering a loop you can see the leading runners coming towards you. But there is also the advantage that after the turn of the loop you can have a look at the slower runners behind you. Such places give Marathon runners the chance to play a psychological game, checking

up on themselves as they compare themselves with the other runners: "Am I doing better than them?"

The route passes through Barcelona's historic old center and then goes slightly uphill for about a mile towards the finishing line. This short distance uphill would be nothing at the start of the Marathon but now it is another matter: the runners are on their last legs, suffering beneath the blazing sun. After passing the statue of Christopher Columbus, every uphill step is agony: spectators will learn a lot of Spanish and Catalan curses from the amateur runners. Then at last there is the high point of the race: the finish on the Plaça d'Espanya.

Spanish oranges

The finishing line is in the square directly below Montjuïc Castle. The relaxed atmosphere is enhanced by the lavish architecture and the lush greenery surrounding it. At the end of the Marathon oranges are handed out: they are so refreshing, so sweet and so tasty that soon the last agonizing steps uphill are forgotten. The bottom line is that the dry, mild, spring climate of northern Spain is perfect for a marathon.

Barcelona has a picturesque historic center, amazing art nouveau architecture, a welcoming cafe culture and all the sophistication of a capital. Marathon runners are treated to a magnificent tour of the city in Spain's second-largest marathon.

"I always listen to my coaches. But first I listen to-my-body."
Haile Gebrselassie

INFORMATION

DATE Mid-March

PARTICIPANTS About 12,000 starters

CHARACTER OF THE ROUTE A mainly flat city course with many sights along the way. The trip is easy to organize oneself, but many tour operators also offer attractive all-inclusive deals, some combined with an attractive tourist program. The marathon is in the first division in terms of organization. There is a large marathon exhibition as well as a breakfast run and a pasta party.

ENTRY FEE From about $85 (£50)

THE CITY Barcelona has become a very popular city for its fashionable lifestyle, its art and its music. The marathon is less important than in some cities, but this is not necessarily a disadvantage for the runner. If you are looking for an event early in the year, with pleasant weather and interesting surroundings, Barcelona is the place.

TIP FOR RUNNERS Barcelona offers an appealing combination of sightseeing and jogging, Sight-Jogging with an accompanying guide. The route is lined with thousands of enthusiastic spectators.

CONTACT DETAILS

Zurich Marató de Barcelona
Gran Via 8–10, 6ª planta
08902 Hospitalet de Llobregat, Barcelona
Spain
Tel.: +34/920/43 17 63
Fax: +34/93/422 10 96
E-Mail: info@zurichmaratobarcelona.es
Internet: www.zurichmaratobarcelona.es

Kilimanjaro Marathon

So close to the summit

Mount Kilimanjaro is the highest mountain in Africa and it has an incredible appeal. With an altitude of 19,341 ft (5,895 m) it rises majestically above its surroundings. It is massive, awe-inspiring and challenging—not least for the Marathon runners who race around the foot of the great mountain.

Snow on Kilimanjaro. From a distance it looks peaceful and inviting (top). But the ascent is demanding, just like the Marathon itself (center). The reward is the view of the exotic (bottom).

There are several mountains that are higher, with more dramatic ascents and steeper slopes. But few rise as spectacularly from the surrounding landscape as Kilimanjaro, which is the highest mountain in the African continent, 19,341 ft (5,895 m) high. It is also one of the few places in Africa with snow and a temperature that is consistently below freezing point. Ambitious mountaineers who are interested in climbing Kilimanjaro will need patience, perseverance and good planning; and even more importantly, a good guide.

The climber will cross five climate zones in the ascent. Although it is not an extreme mountaineering challenge, many climbers fail to reach the summit because of the climate and the altitude. The mountain's beauty is due to its particular location: Kili, as the mountain is familiarly known, is an extinct volcano and there no other mountains of similar size nearby. Since it is free-standing, Mount Kilimanjaro looks particularly impressive. At the foot of the mountain the Tanzanian heat is stifling, while at the summit it is bitterly cold. Temperature differences of over 120° F (50° C) are common.

Through coffee and bananas
The mountain also has an effect on the runners in the Marathon. Although those taking part in the Kilimanjaro Marathon in Tanzania only see the snowy peaks from the foothills, at least preparation for the race is easier in terms of clothes for the climate than it is for climbers aiming to reach the summit.

In the morning when the Marathon starts it is still pleasantly cool, but later on in the race the temperature rises to 86° F (30° C) or more. The start and finish are in the stadium in Moshi, a lively little town whose inhabitants make their living from coffee farming. The route starts in Moshi and goes to Dar es Salam, Tanzania's seat of government, and then back again. After 19.88 miles (32 km), near the locality of Mweka, the runners are faced with a long climb. At its highest point the route reaches an altitude of 4,921 ft (1,500 m) before descending again in the last 5 miles (8 km), making it a pleasant downhill finish for the runners. As they climb the slopes the runners will enjoy the sight of Kili with its snowy peak.

The atmosphere is cheerful and good-humored with the spectators cheering the participants and egging them on. Children often run a few steps with the runners. One senses that they are already dreaming of taking part themselves when older. And here lies the particular attraction of this African Marathon. No one comes only for the Marathon: everyone is here to enjoy the atmosphere of the country and the magnificent mountain. The Marathon route runs through coffee plantations, past small farmers tending their fields, through banana plantations and through forests. But it also often runs through open terrain with no protection from the sun. After this the runners will enjoy the invigorating coolness of the plantations all the more, encouraged by the ever joyful, positive mood of the spectators. Warm-hearted, they always cheer the runners and spur them on, psyching them up with anything that makes a racket.

Out of Africa

Anyone who goes to Tanzania will already have a good idea of the beauty of Africa that has been captured so often in numerous television programs and movies. The key phrase is "Out of Africa." The race is like an invitation to get to know the country and its people.

"Running teaches us to accept what the day brings, what the body allows and what the will permits."
John Bingham

INFORMATION

DATE March

PARTICIPANTS About 300 starters

CHARACTER OF THE ROUTE A demanding marathon that is accompanied by numerous fringe events. One should not be fooled by the locals who are acclimatised but instead let yourself be guided by the few Europeans who are there. The route is mountainous and it can become very hot during the race.

ENTRY FEE About $70 (£40)

THE REGION Whether in the Serengeti National Park or in the Ngorongoro Crater Conservation Area, in Tanzania the traditional safari is a must. It is best to book an organized tour in advance. As part of an official tour you will save yourself the worry of wondering which way to go, you can leave price negotiationsto to others and you will avoid misunderstandings over language.

TIP FOR RUNNERS Pace yourself. The first half should be run in the knowledge that you will then be running 12.04 miles (21 km) back the start. You will then have enough strength for the second half.

CONTACT DETAILS

Wild Frontiers (Pty) Ltd
Registered Member of SATOA
P.O. Box 844
Halfway House 1685
South Africa
Tel.: +27/11/702 20 35
Tel.: +27/72/927 75 29
Fax: +27/86/689 67 59
E-Mail: reservations@wildfrontiers.com
Internet: www.kilimanjaromarathon.com

Two Oceans Marathon

Between the oceans

Exaggeration is common in everyday speech, but here the word "Marathon" is an understatement. With a length of 34.8 miles (56 km) the Two Oceans Marathon is far longer than the standard marathon. It is also one of the most beautiful in the world.

The spectacular route is exhausting but it is rewarded by unique experiences, such as the road section on Chapman's Peak. The marathon is very popular among South Africans and attracts many amateurs as well as top runners.

South Africa has a very active running program and a large number of admirable running events. This may have started with Anglo-Saxon influence introducing its running traditions, but the South African running scene has certainly developed its own momentum. Endurance sports are extremely popular in this beautiful country, which is certainly worth a visit all year round. Tourists from the United States and Europe will be aware that they are travelling to the southern hemisphere, so the climate of the seasons is the opposite of the one they have left. The South African summer takes place when it is winter in the northern hemisphere.

A vibrant running scene

South Africa's spring and autumn months are perfect for a holiday there. There is very little rain in January and February and the weather can be really warm. It is also the period of the grape harvest that is so important in South Africa, attracting more tourists than all the country's sports events put together. The wine industry thrives here with its cool winters, dry soil, sunny weather and adequate rainfall.

Some of the oldest wine-growing estates are in the area where the Two Oceans Marathon is run, the area to the south of Table Mountain, in the Constantia Valley. In March the weather turns cooler and the temperature ranges between 59°F and 77°F (15°C and 25°C). The climate is often compared to that of the Mediterranean. These pleasant weather conditions, combined with the amazingly beautiful scenery, attract not only runners but also numerous other sportsmen: mountain bikers, cyclists and many golfers.

A bonus is that anyone interested in taking part in a run is really spoilt for choice. For instance, the Comrades Marathon is the world's oldest ultra-marathon, founded in 1921, with a length of 55.3 miles (89 km). It is extremely popular, particularly with local runners. The Comrades Marathon is in winter while the Two Oceans Marathon takes place in late summer, which is an advantage: the

running conditions are rather better at that time of the year.

It is not for nothing that Nelson Mandela called his country "The Rainbow Nation." Because of the route's closeness to the ocean, there is no guarantee that the sun will shine. But what is guaranteed is the great atmosphere among the runners. There is a danger that the runners may be carried away by a feeling of euphoria, or in other words: they may be running too fast.

Challenging times ahead
The start is early, at about half past six when it is still dark. At first the route is flat, winding its way through various suburbs. But watch out: people entering the race should be well prepared and know what they are letting themselves in for. In addition to the length of the route, the level of difficulty is particularly high in the second half of the race, with numerous hills, differences in level, trails and non-rhythmical running conditions. In the first half of the race, many of the large number of runners tend to start much too fast and fail to find a rhythm. Soon many will end up in a conversation with their South African co-runners, who are always very ready to talk, chatting away and

The start takes place at dawn as the sun rises on the horizon. The Two Oceans Marathon cannot guarantee fine weather, but when the sun shines it does so with tremendous force.

This is an attractive run for the variety of of scenery that the route passes through. The whole length of the route is lined with spectators whose enthusiastic support expressed in various ways is welcomed by the runners.

forgetting about the pace at which they are running.

Often a first surprise awaits them after barely a quarter of the total distance, when after Lakeside an insidious south-east wind starts to blow, ruffling the runners' hair and slowing them down. This is the first hint of the power of the surrounding ocean. But it is still early in the race—and as far as the wind is concerned it may be seen as the calm before the storm. There is compensation for the runners when they reach the sea shore after some 9.3 miles (15 km). The beautiful view of the ocean will accompany them for the next 3.1 miles (5 km).

Then things become more difficult. Since it is an ultra-marathon, much less than half the route has been completed when the half-marathon mark is reached. At this point the runners should pace themselves because the more demanding but also more picturesque part of the route is still to come. Spectators show anything but restraint: they encourage the runners and spur them on as if the ascent of Chapman's Peak had already started. Chapman's Peak Drive is a road carved into the sheer rock face of the coast, winding its way along the Atlantic shore. Some 590 ft (180 m) are climbed during the ascent of 3.1 miles (5 km). Even so it is far from being the highest point of the route. After running 18.64 miles (30 km) from the start there is a magnificent view of the sparkling waters of the Atlantic which on many days is still relatively calm and smooth in the morning. Many runners, in fact most of them, slow to a walk as they climb the steep slope knowing

what is still awaiting them. Others use an apparently very successful run-walk rhythm that enables them to climb the steep hill yard after yard without interruption.

Then the route descends almost brutally and steeply downhill along the coastline until Hout Bay. Here too the runners must watch their pace, because running downhill too fast can be dangerous. In Hout Bay the spectators provide a welcome diversion. Here there is the heartening spectacle of a wide range of food on offer, such as chocolate, fruit gums, biscuits, potatoes and ice cream. This is heaven-sent for the runners since the route ahead is uphill again and they will need the extra calories. They are about to tackle the steep ascent to Constantia Nek—the highest point of the route at 28.6 miles (46 km) on the inland side of Table Mountain. Here 705 ft (215 m) are climbed over 2.5 miles (4 km).

The runners hardly notice the marathon mark as they pass it, endeavoring not to dwell on the ascents ahead. For many runners this is one of the hardest tests. At the summit there is a control station where many a runner has been taken out of the race against their will but for their own good.

Hill after hill

But again and again the route compensates for its tough conditions. In Kirstenbosch the Botanical Garden with its dense foliage provides welcome shade, much appreciated by the runners. Then in the last phase of the race the runners will really notice the increasing heat. There are only 3.73 miles (6 km) to go and there are now aid and refreshment stations at every kilometer mark. The handing-out of water and other drinks in small plastic sachets is very well organized. When they reach the finish at the Upper

Campus of the University of Cape Town, the runners are rewarded by a magnificent panoramic view. The race is run from gun to gun, that is, it is ended punctually by the firing of a gun exactly 7 hours after the starting gun. Anyone still running is deemed to have retired. Also runners are retired during the race if they have not passed cut-off points within the specified times. In the last ten minutes of the race hundreds of runners dash to cross the finishing line in time. It is spectacular—a real last minute panic!

The Two Oceans Marathon is not a marathon in the literal sense of the word because the route is longer. But the name "Two Oceans" is appropriate since the route includes fantastic views of both the Atlantic and the Indian Oceans. It fully justifies its motto "The world's most beautiful marathon."

> *"Through running I have learnt valuable lessons. Since cross-country training counted more than talent, I was able to compensate for the lack of natural talent with hard work and discipline. This lesson I have heeded in everything I have done."*
>
> *Nelson Mandela*

INFORMATION

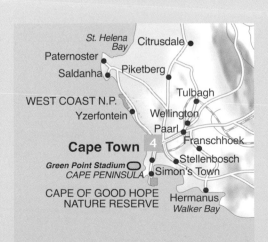

DATE Always on Easter Saturday

PARTICIPANTS About 9,000 starters

Map labels: St. Helena Bay · Citrusdale · Paternoster · Piketberg · Saldanha · Tulbagh · WEST COAST N.P. · Yzerfontein · Wellington · Paarl · Franschhoek · **Cape Town** 4 · Green Point Stadium · CAPE PENINSULA · Simon's Town · Stellenbosch · CAPE OF GOOD HOPE NATURE RESERVE · Hermanus · Walker Bay

CHARACTER OF THE ROUTE Run for the first time in 1970, the Ultramarathon is 34.8 miles (56 km) long and reaches a height of no less than 14,925 ft (1,501 m) with a cumulative drop of 4,708 ft (1,435 m). Starters must have achieved a marathon time of less than 5 hours. At the same time there are various other events in the program including a very attractive half-marathon. The mood is friendly throughout. But the unique scenic experience can only be enjoyed in the long distance event.

ENTRY FEE About $125 (£75)

THE CITY Cape Town itself is barely touched by the marathon since the routes runs only through the suburbs, not through the center. The description chosen by the organizers, "The

most beautiful marathon in the world," is a fair description of the coastal areas and their varied characteristics.

TIPS FOR RUNNERS The Friendship Run the day before takes in the numerous attractions of Cape Town, and it fully justifies the chorus of enthusiasm for this city at the foot of Table Mountain. It is well-named.

CONTACT DETAILS
Old Mutual Two Oceans Marathon
P O Box 2276
Clareinch, 7740
South Africa
Tel.: +27/21/657 51 40
E-Mail: info@twooceansmarathon.org.za
Internet: www.twooceansmarathon.org.za

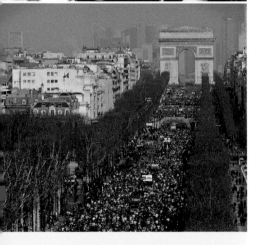

A gloriously impressive start (bottom) , for both runners and spectators. The start fills the entire width of the Avenue des Champs-Elysées, with the Arc de Triomphe in the background. The Place de la Bastille (top) is reached after 3.10 miles (5 km).

Paris Marathon

Running with privilege

Paris is one of the largest marathons: with New York, London, Berlin, Tokyo and Chicago, attracting some 40,000 participants. The route is planned so that runners can also enjoy the great visual highlights of the French capital.

About 16,000 participants in the Paris Marathon come from outside France. Like the millions of tourists who flock to Paris, they know there is plenty to see. The list of appealing tourist attractions more than justifies the journey, particularly since the organizers have ensured that the route of the Marathon takes in a large number of interesting places. Paris has countless interesting highlights and it is happy to show them off.

Where to begin? Quite simply, at the foot of the Arc de Triomphe, the very symbol of Paris. This is where the Paris Marathon starts. Right away there is the excitement of running down the Champs-Élysées to the Place de la Concorde. This is a great privilege because, apart from the Tour de France, this prestigious boulevard is hardly ever closed to traffic.

The mother of all Boulevards
Most importantly, unlike the Tour de France, the Paris Marathon is an event in which everyone can take part; or at least, everyone who has trained for it and is therefore capable of completing a marathon. Certainly the first section to the Place de la Concorde is exhilarating. The Avenue of the Champs-Élysées is slightly downhill and the pace is a little too fast. Adrenalin levels are high and there is room for everyone. But soon the pace slows down—at least in the main pack.

After the Champs-Élysées the streets become narrower and the runners must run closer together. The pace slows further as the runners pass through the Rue de Rivoli towards the Place de la Bastille. There a tailback starts to form, with people bunching together. And this can happen again until the runners reach the last third of the route. In some places the streets are too narrow to accommodate the many runners with the same time slot. This is a well-known phenomenon in big-city marathons!

There is no doubt that runners in the Paris Marathon must be taken seriously. People who can run the marathon in less than three hours will find that the way in front of them is clear. But for those with a target time of 3:15 onwards, things become tightly bunched. So it is best for runners to accept the

26

crowded conditions and congestion with equanimity and enjoy the beauty and atmosphere of the surroundings.

The Paris Marathon was first held in 1896. On July 19 of that year, 191 runners crossed the finishing line. So Paris started at the same time as Athens, and shortly before Boston, where the first marathon took place on April 19, 1897. But unlike the Boston Marathon, in Paris there was a long interruption in the sequence of events and the Paris Marathon was not held again until September 19, 1976.

Life goes on

As a runner one it is sometimes surprising to pass through normal neighborhoods where instead of crowds of spectators people are getting on with everyday life, for instance wandering in parks like the Bois de Vincennes. Later the runners will pass through the Bois de Boulogne, a popular jogging area: "Of course one always remembers the highlights of the marathon," says the half-French Joëlle Muguet, who has already run three Paris marathons. "It is the perfect opportunity to discover many of the different facets of this multi-cultural city: the Sunday strollers, all dressed up, walking in the park."

Now and then the route follows the Seine, when the Eiffel Tower can be seen in the distance until the runners eventually pass it at 18.01 miles (29 km). This is only surpassed by the approach to the finish along the Avenue Foch and the runners' triumph as they arrive in front of the Arc de Triomphe.

"When I walk in the morning, I make healthier and wiser decisions during the day."
Deena Kastor

INFORMATION

DATE Early April

PARTICIPANTS About 40,000 starters

CHARACTER OF THE ROUTE A mainly flat city circuit with a few up and down stretches, for instance along the Seine with its bridges and underpasses.

ENTRY FEE From $90 (£55)

THE CITY Paris is a truly fascinating capital city with its numerous attractions and contradictions. Whether one is talking about corporate finance, culture, fashion or art—this is where it all happens. Everyone will find something of interest. But it comes at a price, literally: the city is no bargain for tourists. For this reason it is worth reading up about the city before traveling there for useful tips about accommodation and where to eat. Much of Paris has maintained its traditional charm and this is why it is such a pleasant place, much of it on a human scale.

TIP FOR RUNNERS Because of the large number of number of participants, you must be patient and allow more time than usual for everything, including getting to the start. There can be congestion in some places on the route.

CONTACT DETAILS

A.S.O. Athlétisme
253 Quai de la Bataille de Stalingrad
TSA 61100
92137 Issy-les-Moulineaux Cedex
France
Tel.: +33/1/41 33 15 68
E-Mail: parismarathon@aso.fr
Internet: www.parismarathon.com

Zurich Marathon

The mountains are here as a backdrop

When Switzerland is mentioned, most people think immediately of the Alps, and indeed Zurich is surrounded by beautiful mountain scenery. But surprisingly, the Zurich Marathon is completely flat with a fast route along Lake Zurich.

Zurich combines tradition and modernity. From the start in the Old Town the course runs over the sweeping Quaibrücke bridge (bottom). In the background are the Women's Minster church and St. Peter's church with the largest clockface in Europe.

The Swiss are thought of as a courteous, rather reserved people. But as in many countries, and like all who live in big cities, the people of Zurich have developed a character of their own. So there is no reserve when the inhabitants of Zurich confidently promote this event as "The marathon in people's favorite city in the world." In the northern part of the country, Zurich is a global city with a large financial center and it has been described as "People's favorite city to live in" for its political stability, its healthcare, its housing situation and its excellent restaurants as well as its incomparable cultural and leisure facilities. The Zurich Marathon is justifiably promoted with the slogan "Best time of your life."

A free panorama

Unlike other Swiss running events such as the Bern Grand Prix, the Zurich Marathon does not have a long history. It has only been going since 2003. It was the brain child of Bruno Lanfranchi, a man known for his endurance and determination who had to fight a tough battle for the project to be accepted.

The former world class runner and Swiss record-holder created a course that went round the city center of the commercial capital, most of it following the shores of Lake Zurich.

The start at the Mythen-Quai is a little away from the center on the west side of the lake. Here the atmosphere is extremely lively because the number of runners entered in the Marathon, between about 2,500 and 3,500, is increased many times over by others who are taking part in the "Teamrun" and the "Cityrun" over 6.2 miles (10 km). First included in the program in 2012, the Cityrun has breathed new life into this running event.

Running is a popular sport in Switzerland and many enthusiasts take the opportunity to enjoy this attractive lake course along the lake with its panoramic views, for instance along the General-Guisan-Quai on the north shore and across the impressive Quaibrücke bridge. Crossing this, the runners reach the west shore. Those taking part in the Cityrun accompany the marathon runners as far Bellerivestrasse, one of the most expensive residential areas in Zurich, before turning off to the left and running back to the city center again. There are a number of popular places where spectator gather, the cheerful atmosphere being enhanced by bands playing all kinds of music.

It is a great experience for the runners who can enjoy the combination of the spectators' enthusiasm and the magnificent views along the lake shore. The marathon route passes through the districts of Küsnacht, Erlenbach and Herrliberg.

Along the gold coast

The turning-point is in Meilen. Here it becomes apparent why this part of the lakeside is known as the "Gold Coast." Poor people do not live here. Meilen also has one of many attractive sandy beaches, bathed in the afternoon sun. For the rest of the marathon the sun shines on the runners from behind. In the words of the Luxembourg runner Joelle Geiben who took part in 2011: "On the way back the Bellerivestrasse stretches out beautifully in front us; on the way out it had looked much shorter." As the runners reach the bendy final stretch through the city center, 2.5 mile (4 km) long, the runners are encouraged by the bustling atmosphere and the spectators.

Some runners occasionally complain about the running surfaces: there are some sections with paved with cobblestones which after 24.9 miles (40 km) can be quite painful. But that is soon forgotten on reaching the final stretch. The view is unforgettable, as is the sense of achievement.

"May the road welcome you and may the wind always blow from behind you."
Irisches Sprichwort

INFORMATION

DATE First half of April

PARTICIPANTS About 3,000 starters

CHARACTER OF THE ROUTE A flat city circuit along the shores of Lake Zurich and through the city center. There is also an interesting event for those who do not want to take part in the marathon because they can take part in the short "City Run." Another possibility is to follow the marathon as a spectator from a boat on Lake Zurich. This is fascinating from a tourist point of view.

ENTRY FEE From $105 (£62)

THE CITY Admittedly Zurich is not the capital of Switzerland but from an international and tourist point of view, it has many of the same characteristics. The cultural diversity, the lively nightlife and the numerous tourist attractions make it well worth visiting when traveling there for the marathon. Zurich is a financial center and this is unfortunately reflected in very high prices, even for the Swiss.

TIP FOR RUNNERS Participants must be prepared for all weather conditions. On the shores of Lake Zurich the weather in spring can be warm and sunny but it can also be windy, cool and rainy.

CONTACT DETAILS
Verein Zürich Marathon
Spindelstraße 2
8041 Zürich
Switzerland
Fax +41/44/480 25 56
E-Mail: info@zuerichmarathon.ch
Internet: www.zurichmarathon.ch

North Pole Marathon

The world's coolest marathon

Here runners will experience the fascination of the Arctic. In the North Pole Marathon there is nothing to disturb the unique symbiosis of nature and the pleasure of running, and perhaps polar bears will be seen. The temperatures can be as low as -22°F (-30°C).

The journey to the North Pole Marathon is almost as challenging as the race itself. Here masked figures are fighting their way through ice and snow simply to reach the start. More than anywhere, the main thing is being there.

The North Pole Marathon is a polarizing event, in the literal sense of the word. It is not for ordinary runners. Those taking part are absolute marathon enthusiasts and extreme runners who want to include this marathon in their list of exceptional sporting achievements. And not surprisingly it is a marathon enthusiast and extreme runner who created the North Pole Marathon, the Irish runner Richard Donovan. He was the first man to run a marathon on both the North Pole and the South Pole and he has now organized marathons in the Arctic and the Antarctic.

It is hard to decide whether a marathon at the top or at the bottom of the globe is the more attractive. The South Pole marathon has slightly better weather, if "better" makes sense in this context. It can be as warm as 14°F (-10°C), which is after all an acceptable running temperature, reached in numerous marathons such as those in Greenland, the Alps or Scandinavia, as well as in the popular winter marathons of Arolsen in Sauerland and the Zurich marathon.

Running on the ice

For lovers of extreme cold weather and of the exotic, there is only one choice: the North Pole Marathon. It is not run in a real place but at the geographical point defined as the North Pole. The surface is just drifting ice. Beneath it lies the Arctic Ocean 13,000 ft (4,000 m) deep. The marathon takes place on an ice sheet with a thickness varying between 6 ft 6 in and 13 ft (2 m and 4 m) that is constantly moving through the Arctic. The North Pole Marathon is the only marathon that is run on water, albeit frozen. The marathon distance is covered on ice that is itself moving. But the runners will not be aware of this because the ice floe on which they are running is so gigantic. In fact it can move at a rate of 1,100 yards (0.5 km) in an hour.

It was in 2003 that Donovan made his first reconnaissance trip with a few intrepid and experienced marathon runners, including the two Austrian runners Helmut Linzbichler and Wolfgang Schwarzäugl.

The year before, after taking part in the South Pole Marathon, he

completed a North Pole Marathon almost solo. In doing this he equaled the achievement of the extravert American extreme runner Dean Karnazas, who until then was the only person to have run a marathon on both Poles. Based on his adventures and his wealth of experience, the charismatic Donovan started his company Polar Running Adventures—the name says it all.

Problems in the cold and ice

A runner who is fascinated by the North Pole must plan the marathon very carefully in every detail. The first essential is to plan financially. The marathon costs about $16,500 (£10,000), including the journey from Longyearbyen on the island of Spitsbergen to the camp near the North Pole, Camp Barneo. The flight to Spitsbergen from the Norwegian mainland is additional, and of course traveling there from the United States or Europe is extra as well. After taking equipment, food and so forth into account, you should allow about $25,000 (about £16,000)—that should see you through.

The route takes in Spitzbergen and Camp Barneo (top). This in itself is quite an experience with a fascinating play of light and extreme climatic conditions. Special running clothing are essential.

The course is circular and each lap is short, so no one can get lost. But recognizing the runners wrapped up agianst the cold is not easy. Fortunately, each runner wears a bib number so it can be established which hooded figure crossed the finish line first .

Here is another tip. Be prepared to stay a little longer in Spitsbergen. Several times in the history of the North Pole Marathon—in 2008 for instance—participants have had to spend several days in Spitsbergen because their aircraft could not yet land at Camp Barneo. The landing strip there has to be built from scratch every year and it was not ready yet. Here the marathon organizers have to face quite unconventional challenges. Unlike most places, parked cars are not a problem, but the ancient Russian tractors used to build a landing strip for the plane in the snow have to be flown here specially by helicopter. Then they have to be started, which can be a problem in itself with old diesel engines at a temperature of -22°F (-30°C), as it was in 2008. From Camp Barneo on the drift ice at the 89th parallel, the runner is flown by helicopter to the 90th parallel, the North Pole. All in all, it is an exciting journey in the strange universe of the fascinating Arctic. And although not a single step has yet been run, the adrenalin is pumping away.

Large running shoes and a triple layer of clothes.

Running here is a completely new experience. There are marshals with guns in case polar bears came too close. The dry snow is brittle. There are cracks in the snow and sharp-edged spikes of ice. Unlike a peaceful frozen pond in winter, the North Pole is formed by drift ice. Ocean currents constantly create new ice formations

that can be as much as 100 ft (30 m) high, but these are not included in the run. Because the snow is powdery, many runners opt for snowshoes that gives more grip on the snowy surface as well as a larger footprint. Another advantage is that they will often save runners from twisted ankles or even falling. But sometimes falls do happen.

The marathon time is of secondary importance: here what counts is the experience. So it is essential to have the right equipment for the polar climate and the snow and ice. Running shoes which must be big enough for two pairs of socks to be worn on top of each other. The running socks themselves are just as important, specially designed and tested for the purpose. As far as the clothes are concerned, every runner must devise a clothes "system." The various layers of clothes must be perfectly coordinated to withstand the cold. As absurd as it may sound, it is important to avoid getting too hot while running. This is because sweating produces moisture and this allows the body heat to escape. The air within the clothes works like an insulator, so anyone who feels pleasantly warm at the start of the race is definitely too warmly dressed—and will later feel all the colder. Stopping at refreshment stations, the blood circulation slows down and the icy cold becomes increasingly palpable.

When running in very cold weather conditions, it is important to work out good customized "rules" for clothes. Many runners opt for three layers of high-quality clothing. First is a base layer that is worn next to the skin and clings evenly to it. This layer is designed to keep the body dry. On top of the base layer the runner wears a warming layer such as a micro-fleece. Then there is the protective outer layer consisting of a functional jacket. Here too one needs to be careful because in polar conditions the usual membrane jacket worn for the winter in more temperate regions will not work very efficiently. With the icy external temperatures it is vitally important that there should be no gaps anywhere exposing bare skin or letting the cold wind blowin.

Richard Donovan has developed his own range of protective garments for the UVU ("You Versus You") clothes brand.

Frozen energy bars

Other aspects of planning have to be carefully worked out too—such as one's own provisions. Energy bars cannot be eaten in this icy weather, because they freeze. So you should consider carefully what you choose to sustain you and test everything in freezing weather conditions. Dried fruit bars are a good choice since they are easy to chew and can be warmed up in a pocket by body heat.

There is plenty of time to chat about all this during the journey to the start of the Marathon. Indeed, a special kind of a camaraderie develops between runners on the way there since they all share the same interests. This is not surprising, since only 50 participants will gather on the starting line.

"Have no fear of the difference between dreams and reality. What you can dream , you can do also."

Unbekannt

INFORMATION

DATE April

PARTICIPANTS About 40 starters

CHARACTER OF THE ROUTE A round circuit at the Pole! A circle of 2.48 (4 km) is marked in the ice so that the runners can stop often at the catering tent.

ENTRY FEE From $16,500 (£10,000)

THE REGION Planning the journey to this region at is a massive project in itself, as is the training needed to run in this marathon. This includes preparatory trips in cold climates to test the equipment throguhly and to train your own body for the harsh conditions. A journey to the North Pole is not to be made on your own, but only as part of an expedition with experienced companions.

TIP FOR RUNNERS Fitness-wise the race is very demanding but not impossible. Strong mental stamina is required, as is a well-thought-out equipment list, including food for the journey. The physical demands are considerable. It is necessary to keep the body warm and also to warm the air that is breathed. As in any marathon, it is essential not to start of too fast. It is very important to pace yourself, especially on the ice or the soft substratum.

CONTACT DETAILS

Richard Donovan
Polar Running Adventures
95 Rosan Glas – Rahoon Road
Galway / Irland
Tel. & Fax: + 353/91/51 66 44
E-Mail: rd@npmarathon.com
Internet: www.npmarathon.com

Vienna Marathon

There's music everywhere

It is not surprising that Vienna, the capital of Austria, attracts tourists like a magnet since is one of Europe's most important cultural cities. While being steeped in history and tradition, it is also important today for its political and cultural influence. And the Vienna Marathon is a very good reason to go to Vienna and discover its pleasures.

Many of the 30,000 runners in the Vienna Marathon come from other countries to take part in the event. The Austrians too take advantage of the marathon to come and visit their capital in large numbers. No one can fail to be impressed by the magnificence of the City of Music, especially when the weather is pleasant, as it has been most times in the last 20 years. When the sun shines the marathon runners are like a sightseeing group in running shoes, so long as their legwork has left them with enough breath and concentration to notice the beautiful sights along the route.

To the Prater at the double
In the first 2.5 miles (4 km) the runners cross the bridge from the modern to the traditional. The marathon starts on Danube Island in the heart of the city's economic center. Here futuristic high-rise buildings such as the UN headquarters flank the starting line. The runners wait at the start, tightly packed

together. After the starting signal, the runners immediately set off on the long Reichsbrücke across the Danube, or to be exact across the Danube canal, over Danube Island and then across the River Danube itself. As they cross, Danube Island can be seen on the left and right while ahead of them lies the old town and the city center of Vienna.

But just before the runners reach the center of the city, the route diverts towards the Prater, Vienna's large public park that is one of the most beautiful in the world. The amusement park there is open all year round and in it is the giant Ferris wheel that is one of the highlights on the marathon route, famous for its appearance with Orson Welles in the movie The Third Man. All over the Prater the chestnut trees are in bloom, a beautiful sight. The cafés and kiosks in the park tempt the Sunday wanderers to come and relax while others are walking their "Schnauferl"—the Viennese word

The start seen from Danube Island (top) as the runners cross the bridge between the modern and traditional parts of the city. The old town is full of historic monuments such as the Ringstrasse and the Parliament building (center).

for a little dog. So only a few people pay any attention to the marathon runners.

Fast novices

But this changes suddenly as soon as the runners reach the magnificent boulevard of the Ringstrasse. Here numerous groups of spectators have gathered below the magnificent historic buildings, along Linke Wienzeile and Mariahilfer Strasse. The many music bands lining the route encourage the runners. The reputation of the marathon has grown considerably in recent years and many Viennese now take part in associated events, including children's races and relay events.

The marathon is also known for the number of elite runners who take part. These include well-known runners who have made a name for themselves in long distance races but have never run a marathon. As result the Vienna marathon has become a popular marathon for people who are technically novices. But because the organizers are successful in attracting elite runners, competitors also include old hands such as the world record holders Haile Gebreselassie and Paula Radcliffe.

The first half of the route is the same as that followed by the half-marathon and it runs mainly through the inner city area and popular neighborhoods. The second part is perhaps a little less picturesque, but the final part along the Opernring and the Burgring with a truly royal finale at the Heldenplatz is more than compensation. A worthy finish for the heroic runners.

"I prefer to run without shoes. If one in is the lead right from the start, no one can tread on your feet."

Mary Dekkers

INFORMATION

DATE Mid-April

PARTICIPANTS About 9,000 starters

CHARACTER OF THE ROUTE The city circuit is mostly flat but there are a few gentle uphill stretches. The route takes the runners past many of the interesting sites in and around the center of the city: the Opera House, the spectacular Palace of Schönbrunn, the Prater with its Ferris wheel and the Rathaus. Fast times are possible on this route. The marathon finishes in the magnificent Heldenplatz in front of the Hofburg Palace.

ENTRY FEE From $85 (£50)

THE CITY Vienna has always been a melting pot of many nations and cultures. This is still true today and it is what gives the city its character and charm. There are numerous cultural events for visitors to the city. And visitors will discover the true meaning of having "enough time" in the city's many traditional coffee houses.

TIP FOR RUNNERS Danube Island and the banks of the Danube provide a delightful running track. For training you can vary your route as the mood takes you. Those who prefer the mountains have an alternative: the nearby Vienna Woods with beautiful nature trails.

CONTACT DETAILS
Enterprise Sport Promotion
Gußhausstraße 21/19
1040 Wien
Austria
Tel.: +43/820/99 09 12
Fax: +43/1/606 95 10 40
Internet: www.vienna-marathon.com

Start and finish. The route of the Boston Marathon is a point-to-point course, so the start and the finish are in different places. This is for historic reasons and it has always been the case since 1896. Similarly, it is always held on a Monday.

Boston Marathon
Back to the beginnings

The Boston Marathon is intimately involved in the history and legend of marathon running, and it is correspondingly popular. It is a unique marathon and taking part in it is a unique experience that will be long remembered.

The Boston Marathon has been held every year since 1897 and it has almost always followed the same route. It has never been dropped or cancelled. There are countless stories and impressive facts associated with it. Bill Rodgers, who has won four times in Boston as well as four times in New York, described it as follows: "I have always believed that the marathon is the supreme discipline in sport. And naturally, Boston is the king of marathons." This race reflects the history of running more than any other. From the world's best performance to age group records, from the history of amateur sport to professional sport and the commercialization of the running discipline: Boston has always been at the forefront.

The history of the marathon
The Boston Marathon tells us much about the origin of this running discipline. Looking back, the Athens Olympic Marathon in 1896 was originally planned as a one-off event. This was how the Frenchman Michel Bréal saw it: for the 1896 Olympic Games in Athens, he had suggested a commemorative run in honor of the messenger Pheidippides who in 490 BC had run from the Battle of Marathon to Athens with the news that the Greeks had defeated the Persians. This idea of a commemorative run was received enthusiastically, even though it was by then known that the tale of Pheidippides was a myth: as one might say, it deserved to be true. Bréal suggested the idea to Baron Pierre de Coubertin and he very generously wanted to donate a Cup for the run.

Then the story of the Marathon became a sure-fire success when on April 10, 1896, a suntanned Greek wearing a white tunic was the first man to enter the Olympic stadium in Athens in front of 70,000 euphoric spectators. The wave of patriotic enthusiasm in Greece was accompanied by international media interest.

The winner of the first Olympic Marathon was Spiridon Louis and his victory was widely reported by the international press.

As a result, plans to organize their own marathon races spread throughout the countries of Europe and the United States.

Boston thrives on the tradition and so do the runners. The race always takes place on Patriots' Day, the third Monday in April. Many runners will be remembering 2013, the victims of the terrible attack (center).

Notably, there was great interest in Boston on the East Coast of the United States where a few athletes who had taken part in the Athens Olympic Games lived. They elaborated the legend and related it to their own history. The first Boston Marathon took place in 1897 and was staged in honor of the classic rides of Paul Revere and William Dawes. On April 19, 1775, during the American War of Independence, the two men had ridden through the night to warn the people of Massachusetts of the British attack. Thus Patriot's Day appeared to be the perfect date for the American commemorative run. So here again the marathon was founded on a good story.

A record course

It would have added a further historic dimension to the event if the course of the Boston Marathon had followed the route of the nocturnal ride of Revere and Dawes, since its purpose was so similar to that of the messenger Pheidippides. But this did not happen, partly because the precise historic route was not entirely known and the streets had changed. The course today is a point-to-point one starting in the town of Hopkinton, to the west of Boston. Every year the organization of the marathon is a mammoth logistical task for the organizers and it also requires efficient preliminary planning on the part of the runners.

Seen on paper the course is easily underestimated, its finish line being 460 ft (40 m) lower than the start line. This contributed to Geoffrey Mutai running the fastest marathon race ever recorded with a time of 2:03:02 hours in 2011.

But because of the elevation drop, the Kenyan's record was not recognized as a world record. The maximum elevation drop allowed on a point-to-point course is 1 percent of the total length of the route, that is, 138 ft (42 m). So anyone wanting to set a world record must choose their race with care.

But even more important than the elevation drop was the wind, as it was in 2011. When the wind is favorable, runners benefit from it throughout almost the whole race. But you cannot rely on it. Rain, heat and cold, all these conditions have been experienced in Boston. The times of average runners are therefore usually unremarkable. This is partly due to the fact that some parts of the route are hilly. Heartbreak Hill is legendary: as the runners reach 19.9 miles (32 km), the course suddenly goes uphill. The hill itself is not alarmingly steep, but for runners who are beginning to experience problems, Heartbreak Hill will appear like the north face of the Eiger.

Unforgettable winners

Because of the course is not entirely flat, the many records set here are all the more admirable. For instance, in 1968 Derek Clayton completed the marathon in 2:08:34 hours, a time that had been considered impossible until then. In 1975 the German runner Liane Winter also set a record when she improved her own best time by 8 minutes, completing the race in 2:42:24 hours. In that year Kathrine Switzer, the first woman to run the Boston marathon as a numbered entry, finished second. In 1968 her name had appeared as K. V. Switzer in the list of Boston Marathon runners. But in those days women were not allowed to take part in the marathon. As a result Race Director Jock Semple screamed at Kathrine Switzer: "Get the hell out of my race and give me those numbers." He tried to push her violently out of the race. But the other runners protected Switzer who finished the race. She had set an example. Women were officially allowed to take part for the first time in 1972. In 1984 the marathon also became an Olympic discipline for women. Such stories make the Boston marathon unique. And the winners are never forgotten.

Defying terror

2013 was a memorable year, marked by the terrifying bomb attack near the finish line of the Boston Marathon which killed three people. About 140 people were seriously injured. Not only the running community was shocked. As the sports journalist Michael Reinsch wrote: "The terrorist attacked the very symbol of the spirit of challenge, performance and joy: sport." And it took place at one of the most symbolic marathon venues, during the 117th Boston Marathon.

The reaction of white-haired 78-year old Bill Iffrig reflects the reaction of the runners. He was close to the finish and he fell to the ground when one of the bombs exploded near him. He hit his knee hard but got up immediately and ran to cross the finish line. Many runners praised him for his determination to defy terror. One of the runners wrote in Facebook: "Whoever would challenge the human spirit by attacking marathon runners has chosen the wrong target."

"Winning has nothing to do with the race, but with struggling, optimism and not giving up."

Boston-Marathon-Sieger Amby Burfoot

INFORMATION

DATE The thrid Monday in April, Patriots' Day in Massachusetts

PARTICIPANTS About 25,000 starters

CHARACTER OF THE ROUTE A slightly up and down route, very demanding for insufficiently trained runners. Very important: in order to register you must have a Qualifying Time document. For a man 40 years old, for example, this is 3:15 hours, and for a woman of the same age 3:45 hours. Some tour operators have starting places available for an extra charge, and on balance this is usually the most cost-effective solution. The mood and atmosphere are fantastic regardless of the weather.

THE CITY Boston has a great tradition and is famous for its art, music and culture. Harvard University has a worldwide reputation. The city of Boston gives a delightful impression of America in days gone by.

TIP FOR RUNNERS When preparing for the Boston Marathon runners must definitely spend time training on hilly terrain, especially during the long preparation runs. By doing this Heartbreak Hill will not appear so terrifying any more.

CONTACT DETAILS

Boston Marathon
Hopkinton Office
The Starting Line/One Ash Street
Hopkinton MA 01748
United States of America
Tel.: +1/508/435 69 05
Fax. +1/508/435 65 90
E-Mail: registration@baa.org
Internet: www.baa.org

London Marathon

Very British

You have to be quick for the London Marathon. Not so much in the race itself, because there you have all the time in the world, taking up to nine hours before the marathon closes. But for registration, there are just a few hours to apply before the maximum number of applications is reached. Then the actual participants are selected by ballot. In fact, that says it all about this marathon.

Obligatory sights for every tourist—and every runner: Big Ben (top) and Tower Bridge (bottom). The London Marathon is also a comprehensive sightseeing tour.

Queen Elizabeth in Buckingham Palace lives very close to the marathon finish line. She has never commented on the subject and of course she would never be seen in running shoes. She would have a wonderful view of the finish from her balcony. From a different direction, runners have a fine view of Buckingham Palace as they complete the last few yards of the marathon, in spite of their tunnel vision and low carbohydrate levels.

Top in charitable donations

The London Marathon is one of the top ten events worldwide and in the top three in Europe. In some respects London is unbeaten, for instance in collecting money for charitable purposes. The full name of the event is the Virgin Money London Marathon and in the course of it several million pounds are collected each year. About three-quarters of all the participants are running for charitable organizations and the promoters provide places for this. This tradition started in 1981 when the first London Marathon was organized. Since then over $1,150 million (£700 million) have been collected for charity. This is quite unique in the world of marathon running.

London was a late starter in the round of capital marathons, but it quickly took off and there was no stopping it. In 1981, the first year, 7,747 people took part and in 1982 the number of runners had already risen to 16,000. Running sports have always been popular in United Kingdom so the idea of the London Marathon fell on fertile soil. The event was suggested by Chris Brasher, the athlete who won the 3,000-meter steeplechase (a distance of 1.86 miles) in the 1956 Olympic Games. He had already been one of the two pacesetters for Roger Bannister who in May 1954 was the first person to run a mile in under four minutes. This was the legendary "four minute mile," a performance that at the time

was compared with the first ascent of Mount Everest.

In 1979 Brasher took part in the New York Marathon. It immediately struck him that the concept could be transposed to London: a "running spectacle" that would involve both participants and spectators. It would not be a low-key event through the suburbs but it would be focused on the center of the city.

The atmosphere is a delightful one. Instead of the determined individualism or "man against man" attitude that used to be typical of road running in England, it is a really enjoyable event with thousands of cheering spectators along the route which passes numerous tourist sights.

Tourist sights along the route

Brasher was no mere visionary—he was a doer. And so his idea became a reality and the marathon is a multi-faceted spectacle. The spectators are excited by the sight of the runners and the runners are thrilled by the presence of the cheering spectators as well as their fellow participants. On top of this, the route through London is punctuated by many famous landmarks. Who would not cherish memories of the finish with Buckingham Palace in the background?

Typically British. The marathon runners pass Buckingham Palace just before the finish (top). Also typically British is the custom of dressing up. Runners vie with each other for the most unusual costume (bottom).

Although many World Records have been set in London, the course is not thought to be exceptionally fast. Most runners take part in it for fun, rather than to make the fastest time.

Or delight in picturing themselves running across Tower Bridge?

Anyone who has tried to "do" the city in a weekend knows how difficult it is to see just to see a handful of tourist sights. Everywhere is crowded and the city is very spread out so it takes time to get from one place to another. Admittedly things are also quite tight for the runners themselves. Half the participants take an average of about 4:30 hours to complete the marathon. In doing this they will see quite a lot of sights as they run past them. These will include many that the average tourist will never discover on a weekend break. A prime example is the area round the start of the race in Greenwich Park near the Royal Observatory. So marathon runners can say that they started the race in the morning at the spot that sets the time for all the clocks. When the sun is at its highest over the Greenwich meridian, 0° longitude, it is 12 midday. This is Greenwich Mean Time or GMT. This term is still widely used, although it is now properly referred to as Universal Time Coordinated or UTC. The clocks in London are set to it, so everyone should be on time at the start.

The elite start first

The elite female and male runners start the race separately. This makes sense in several respects in view of the number of top class runners. Every year London attracts some the best elite runners, partly because of its high appearance fees and prize money. So spectators lining the route and viewers watching on television can always enjoy a thrilling race. Above

all, London is a fast marathon, as is illustrated by Paula Radcliffe's world record in 2003 when she completed the race in an incredible 2:15:25 hours. The previous year she had set the women's record in the Chicago Marathon at 2:17:25 hours, 1:30 minutes faster than Catherine Ndereba before her. In 2003 Paula Radcliffe ran the last 875 yards (800 m) in 2:25 minutes. Ten years later the then Race Director and professional marathon runner Dave Bedford described Radcliffe's race as the most magnificent long-distance running performance he had ever seen.

Since then the London Marathon has seen many top performances, helping many runners become stars, such as the runners Katrin Dörre-Heinig (three wins) and Irina Mikitenko (two wins). The best times of the ten fastest runners in London are also usually the fastest worldwide—which says it all about the route, the winners' prize money and the marathon's appeal to elite runners.

The main pack of runners have to take things at a more leisurely pace. In many places the route becomes quite narrow and the runners have to slow down, particularly in the first half. For this reason the organizers have limited the number of runners on the route to 35,000. During the first 1,100 yards (1 km) the field has time to sort itself out. And it is obvious that the wit and humor of the British is as great as their sportsmanship. In fact, many runners are hoping to set unusual records In 2012 alone more than 150 runners tried to get an entry in the Guinness Book of Records, for categories such as being the fastest marathon runner in a Spiderman costume, in a bridal gown, in a diving suit, dressed as a Roman soldier, as a waiter or as an insect. Numerous "animals" take part in the marathon, including hippopotamuses, panthers, gorillas and giraffes.

A royal straight

About halfway through the marathon the Tower of London suddenly comes into view. The runners cross the Thames and the route takes them towards fashionable East London, zigzagging through Docklands and Canary Wharf. Here too there are narrow stretches where runners have to slow down. At this point the 20 mile (32 km) mark is reached, the critical point in a marathon, after which it will become plain who has followed a professional training plan and who has not. Now the direction turns towards the home. At the 24 mile (38.6 km) mark the runners are suddenly motivated. The course it is slightly downhill towards the Blackfriars underpass, then it runs along the river bank, undoubtedly one of the most beautiful stretches, lined with crowds of screaming spectators. It is estimated that there as many as 700,000 people dotted along the entire route. The runners then go past Big Ben, the Houses of Parliament and along Birdcage Walk towards Buckingham Palace. They have now reached the 26 mile (41.8 km) mark. Turning into the Mall at the famous roundabout in front of the Palace they enter the Mall, they run the final straight towards the finish line. A truly royal finish!

"A win is great—but the friendship among runners is greater still."
Emil Zátopek

INFORMATION

DATE April

PARTICIPANTS About 35,000 starters

CHARACTER OF THE ROUTE Because of the demand, there is a lottery for starting positions. The best way to register is through a travel operator who may be able to arrange a place in the Marathon as well as the journey.

ENTRY FEE From $280 (£165)

THE CITY Travel arrangements can be made through a tour operator or individually. A tip for participants and accompanying spectators: on the day of the marathon it is best to buy a 1-Day Travelcard, which gives unlimited travel on both the Underground (the tube) and on buses, because then you are completely flexible. There are very goods apps which will help you work out your route and plan in advance. The Marathon organizers also provide a lot of

information for spectators on their Web site.

TIP FOR RUNNERS The decision to take part in the Marathon should be taken in August or September at the latest, otherwise all the places will be gone. You will find a list of organizers and trqvael operators online; many offer sightseeing tours as well.

CONTACT DETAILS
Virgin Money London Marathon
PO Box 3460
London SE1 0YA
United Kingdom
Tel.: +44/20/79 02 02 00
E-Mail: info@london-marathon.co.uk
Internet: www.virginmoneylondon marathon.com

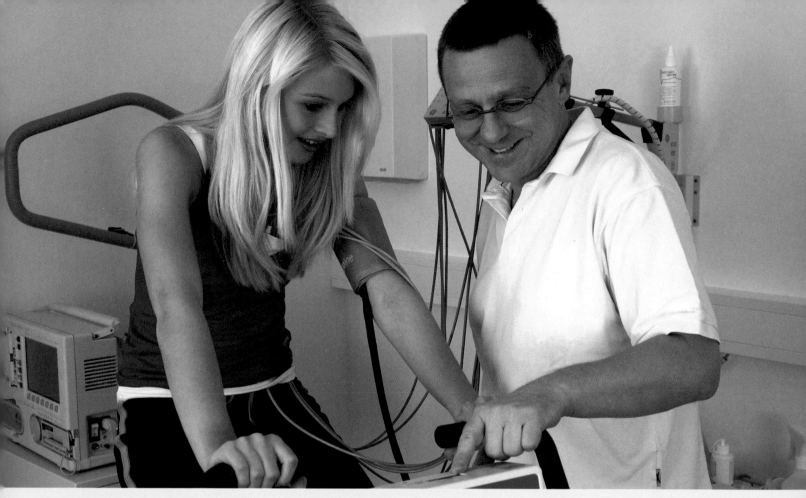

A thorough medical check-up is an essentail part of preparing to run marathons.

Marathons and Health
Who can and who may run a marathon?

The opinions of the Czech long distance runner Emil Zátopek are as follows: "I consider running and especially endurance running the healthiest kind of sport in our modern life. That is why I believe that the marathon is not the most difficult but the most complete sport for the human body and organism."

Running is healthy, and runners are healthier people compared to the average population.

But the decision to run a marathon must be carefully considered and it must include a medical check-up. People whose doctors have recommended taking part in more active sport—as that is the case for many people in modern industrial countries—will almost certainly benefit from running. The positive physical effects of running are multiple. No other sport is so comprehensive and effective

at improving physical condition, for instance by combating excess weight, which it does not only by burning calories but above all by regulating the appetite and attitude to eating in a natural manner. So running helps people lose weight and maintain the loss. Regular running training also regulates blood pressure and cholesterol levels. The "good" cholesterol HDL (high density lipoprotein) increases by

30 percent, while triglyceride levels decreases. By running just over 9 miles (15 km) a week, the risk of high blood pressure or hypertension decreases on average by 39 percent.

Healthy for the body

For people with high blood pressure, running can lower the diastolic pressure by 20 mm Hg and the systolic pressure by 11 mm Hg. These improvements are often enough for many people not to need blood pressure medication. The higher the initial values, the greater the positive effects can be. But scientists have observed widely varying blood pressure developments in similar cases, so people with such problems should be very careful. In general people with a blood pressure above 150/110 mm Hg should have a thorough medical check-up and take their doctor's advice before embarking on running a marathon.

As it happens, the lowering of blood pressure is one of the fastest things to occur during endurance training, usually after just a few weeks. The reason for this is the strengthening of the parasympathetic nervous symptom which reduces the stress hormone. At the same time blood vessel elasticity, water and salt metabolism are regularized, so the reduction of excess weight has a long-term positive effect on the blood pressure.

The good thing about running, and its great advantage compared to other sport disciplines, lies in the relatively small amount of time it takes up. Many of the benefits of running will be felt from running only two hours a week. If all inactive people did some light running training, billions of dollars of health costs could be saved. Cardiovascular diseases would be drastically reduced. It has also been shown that running has a positive effect in relation to some cancers. Women can reduce the risk of developing breast cancer by 30 percent while men who run regularly can reduce the risk of prostate cancer by up to 61 percent.

Beneficial to the psyche

But do not be misled: a marathon race is not run for health reasons in the strict medical sense. It is unlikely that any doctor would advise a patient to run a marathon. It is up to the individual to make the decision and benefit from the positive psychological effect of taking part and the pride taken in one's performance. The willpower and self-confidence that are required have a lasting effect that is surpassed by few other achievements in life.

At the same time, runners should be aware that marathon running can be stressful. So, as for all extreme sports, it is important to have a thorough medical check-up before deciding to take part in a marathon, as mentioned above. People who want to run a marathon need to be physically healthy. Indeed, a medical check-up is obligatory in some countries. Elsewhere, runners should be having a regular health check-up anyway out of personal interest and a sense of responsibility.

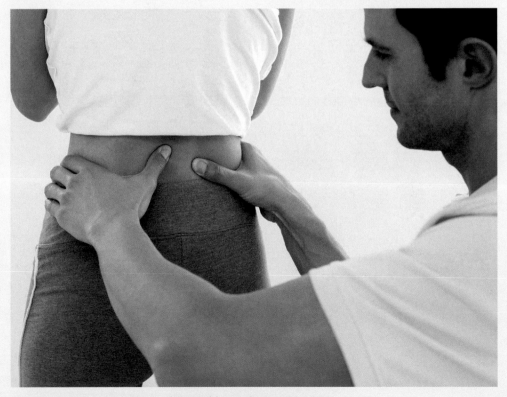

The sports doctor also looks out for possible misalignments.

Running training has far-reaching positive health effects both for the body and for the psyche.

Having said all this, many people with health conditions can run a marathon. For instance, there are many instances of diabetics who have run marathons successfully in spite of their condition: a victory for the mind and for the body. The following should be checked:

- Blood pressure and blood count
- Cardiovascular system
- Orthopedic aspects
- Muscular imbalance
- Stomach and bowels
- Possibly the skin as well

Before the marathon

Even the most talented novice runners cannot undertake a marathon without preparing themselves. The longest journey must start with a few small steps. People should have been running long distances for at least two years before they begin to prepare for a marathon, since this is the time it takes for the whole body to adjust to the stress of endurance running. It is important not to use a sledge-hammer approach. As far as marathon training is concerned, there are no shortcuts.

After the marathon

After the marathon it is absolutely vital to undertake a long phase of regeneration. The muscles can continue to pull for several days and complete recuperation can take up to ten weeks. The rule of thumb is that runners should allow themselves twice as many days for regeneration as they have run miles.

TIPS FROM THE SPORTS DOCTOR

INTERVIEW WITH PROF. DR. BILLY SPERLICH

What medical check-ups are recommended for a runner who wants to run a marathon? What should be checked?

Prof. Dr. Billy Sperlich: That depends on the runner's general health. A young person who has been jogging regularly three times a week and has regular check-ups does not need a special check-up. For older runners who are untrained and/or overweight, I would recommend an exercise echocardiogram. And those who have had orthopedic-related problems should check with an orthopedic specialist as well as a sports doctor.

Are there any pre-existing conditions or illnesses that make it impossible to run a marathon, or can anyone do it?

Sperrlich: If the heart check-up has not revealed any problems and there are no orthopedic injuries, I cannot see any difficulty. But in the event of an acute infection such as a cold there may be problems with immunity, so caution is recommended. Even if it is only a snuffle.

The number of women taking part in marathons is rising. From a medical point of view are there any differences they should take into account in preparing for the marathon and in the marathon itself?

Sperrlich: On the whole no. But there are two things to look out for. First, iron deficiency occurs more quickly. So if a woman feels tired or listless, she should have her iron levels checked. Secondly, women suffer more often from fatigue fracture when they have reached a certain number of miles in training since it is hormone-related.

From a physical point of view, what are the ideal external (climatic) conditions for a marathon?

Sperrlich: Cool and slightly windy! By cool, I mean about 64°F (18°C). Or perhaps I should say from 57 to 64°F (14 to 18°C).
And: No direct sun.
The body dissipates heat best in a light wind.

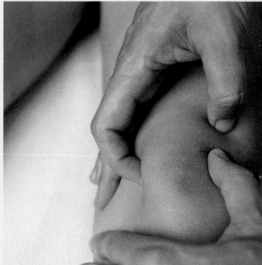

Runners' legs are in the capable hands of sports physiotherapists or orthopedic specialists.

The West Coast of the United States offers impressive landscapes (top and bottom). A pianist at the sode of the track provides background music (center).

Big Sur Marathon

Showdown on Highway 1

One of the most popular dream roads in the world, Highway 1 in California, is closed to the traffic just once a year. This exclusive event is the Big Sur International Marathon, an event that will reward runners with a truly unique experience.

Part of U.S. Route 101, Highway 1 runs along the Pacific coast through countryside that is mostly unspoilt and sparsely populated. It was the first road in the United States to have been awarded the title "Scenic Highway." The part of California where the marathon takes place is a paradise for riders of Harley-Davidsons and drivers of convertibles who love to cruise the highway. As the name suggests, the Marathon starts in Big Sur, a little hamlet far from anywhere with a rich history: it consists of one petrol station and a few holiday houses. But very conveniently it happens to be exactly 26 miles (42 km) south of Carmel on the Monterey peninsula where the marathon finishes.

Monterey and Carmel are about two hours' drive from San Francisco. This is why for many runners the marathon also becomes part of a sightseeing tour. It is a particularly rewarding one because the route goes through one of the most beautiful sections of U.S. Route 101 as it winds its way through several states along the West Coast. Big Sur is situated in one of the protected State Parks that is famous for its impressive giant redwoods, with trunks that often reach a diameter of over 16 ft (5 m). From Big Sur, Highway 1 winds its way, spaghetti-like, along the picturesque Californian west coast.

Coast and sea, cliffs and forest

At the Big Sur International Marathon, the most picturesque of all highways becomes a private running track for a few hours. The destination is famous: very popular in the past with hippies, Carmel is today a fashionable holiday resort, also well-known for its famous golf course on Pebble Beach. This part of the coast is one of the most beautiful and picturesque sections of the whole West Coast. Instead of being lined with skyscrapers—as it is in the big-city marathons in the US—the route is flanked by the sea and beaches, by cliffs and forests. Stretches of coastal scenery alternate with rugged hillsides. There are also 25 bands along the marathon

route, adding to the atmosphere and competing with the thunderous concert of the waves of the Pacific Ocean in the background. The event also attracts many spectators who would not otherwise stray along this stretch.

Piano concert on Bixby Bridge

The bands and solo virtuosos offer a wide range of music. From melodious bel canto to hard rock music, from Dixieland to disco, from rapping school orchestras to the highlight on the Bixby Bridge, a concert pianist wearing a tailcoat, seated at a grand piano. The scene is out of this world and is undoubtedly one of the most extraordinary experiences on the marathon scene, classical music being played on the open-air stage of the marathon route. Here the filigree arch bridge spans the steep Bixby Creek, a popular setting for automobile advertisements. The grand piano is set up at the end of the bridge along the marathon route. A few spectators surround the pianist in tails. An older couple, all dressed up, sit in front of their Rolls Royce, their picnic table set up as they drink a sparkling drink from Champagne glasses. The music

Breathtaking. Bixby Bridge is a highlight of the route (top). The legendary Highway 1 is completely closed to traffic for the duration of the Marathon.

The coast falls steeply to the Pacific Ocean (top) and there are amazing sights to see along the route (center). The mood as runners near the finish is uninhibited (bottom).

rings across the bridge and through the valley: a delightful musical accompaniment for the spectacle of runners.

The runners will also enjoy the Taiko drummers who have taken up position in a valley at the foot of the ascent to Hurricane Point. There they create an echo with their large Japanese drums, making deep vibrations that can be heard by the runners from several miles away: boom, boom, boom—the echoing beats help the runners along, but they cannot "drum away" Hurricane Point. This is highest point of the marathon, at the end of the longest climb, which runs all the way from the first low point of the route, at the Little Sur River Bridge where the Taiko Drummers have taken up position, to Hurricane Point. The long ascent of over 500 ft (150 m) seems like a wall.

It is here at the top of this long climb that the first hints of the outcome of the race start to be seen. And for the runners in mid-field, it is clear that they will not be doing their best time today, since with every upward step the average speed decreases. At the same time, in most years the valley is steeped in a deep silence—apart from the Taiko Drummers. This is in stark contrast with the storm-tossed stretches of the route along the sea and the exposed summit of Hurricane Point, 560 ft (170 m) above sea level. Here the Pacific coast reveals its incredible savagery. In many years it rains and gales are blowing. It certainly gives an idea of how the raging force of the sea has shaped the sheer cliffs along the coast.

Sweet strawberries along the way
Such weather is in stark contrast with the lovely sunny days when the sea lions come and bask on the warm golden sandy beaches, the brass instruments of the musicians sparkle in the sun and the runners can enjoy its warm glow. Good-humored spectators line the route, dressed in the characteristic Californian beach style. Many will offer the runners a specialty of the area: fresh strawberries! For the runners, these are the sweetest, most delicious strawberries one can imagine.

Perhaps they are not the ideal nourishment for a marathon, but on the final stretch they make a welcome change to the energy drink that is handed out at the drinks stands along the route. The strawberries are grown locally and the spectators standing along the route with baskets full of fruit for the runners are typical of the generous Californian spirit. Also typically Californian are the many different forms of encouragement such as posters painted with fanciful representations of the runners, held up by the spectators. These provide a welcome change in the last 5 miles (8 km) of the race as well as a pleasant motivation, since up to this point the route has been through uninhabited countryside. As the route approaches the suburbs of Carmel, individual groups of spectators have gathered together, usually near a music band. Or at a gas station: since there are no cars today, no gas will be sold, so on the spur of the moment the attendant has decided to organize a little marathon party. And reflecting Californian humor, there is a reminder about drinking in moderation, shaped like a skeleton placed on the roadside.

Also striking, shortly before the finish on the left, is the entrance to Point Lobos State Reserve, undoubtedly one of the most beautiful nature reserves in the coastal area. The runners will hardly notice the wooden sign because it is obscured by rows of spectators, some of whom, hippy-like, are dancing barefoot. In Carmel the runners are greeted by more music mingling with the sound of the waves.

The Big Sur International Marathon on Highway 1 is a scenic delight. Neither a Harley Davidson nor an elegant convertible can convey this as well as the marathon runners, who are "Running on the Ragged Edge of the Western World." And for the runners these memories will last forever.

> *"I have no idea how the creative process works. One thing is clear: It always starts when I walk. "*
>
> *Author Robert A. Caro*

INFORMATION

DATE End of April

PARTICIPANTS About 9,000 starters

CHARACTER OF THE ROUTE The Pacific is no lake. The sea is rough and there is a lot of wind, not to mention storms. At Hurricane Point some 550 ft (150 m) of elevation gain are climbed over 2.17 miles (3.5 km). And yet: the famous American running expert Bart Yasso who has himself run numerous marathons throughout the world and knows the scene better than anyone else, said this about the Big Sur Marathon: "If there is one marathon you should run in your life, then it is the Big Sur."

ENTRY COST From $140 (£85)

THE REGION California is—as it always has been —a favorite holiday destination. And rightly too! For lovers of literature, a visit to the authentically designed Henry Miller Memorial library. The cult writer retired to Big Sur in the past where he entertained artists, poets and other writers, including Jack Kerouac who named his novel Big Sur after this place.

TIPS FOR RUNNERS There are delightful runs on the wild nature trails along the Pacific coast or on the beach itself.

CONTACT DETAILS
Big Sur International Marathon
3618 The Barnyard
Carmel, CA 93923
United States of America
Tel.: +1/831/625 62 26
Fax: +1/831/625 21 19
E-Mail: sally@bsim.org
Internet: www.bsim.org

Hamburg Marathon

Arriving at the home port

The Hamburg marathon is definitely worth it. The number of attractions between the start and the finish, together with the enthusiasm of the locals, make this marathon an extraordinary sightseeing tour and an unforgettable experience.paceer

In the Hamburg Marathon the runners pass the city's most important tourist sites of Hamburg, including the Rickmer Rickmers" moored at the pier in St. Pauli (bottom).

When Hamburg invites runners to take part in a marathon, the invitation includes the entire family. The organizers leave no one out. And this has an effect on the atmosphere among runners and spectators. As well as the marathon itself, there are school races, a relay marathon and a 10K marathon. Any Hamburg inhabitant you speak to during the marathon weekend is likely know somebody who is taking part in one of them, and one way and another everyone seems to be connected with the events in some way. Hamburg is often described as Germany's "Gateway to the World," and it is definitely wide open during the marathon weekend.

Over 20,000 runners take part in the various distances. More than 11,000 runners complete the full marathon. This impressive number is 1,000 more than the previous year, and this puts the Hamburg marathon among the winners: most marathons in the Top 20 have recently recorded a drop in the number of participants. So, in the Hanseatic city the field of runners is very tight at all times, but on the whole the runners do not tread on each other's

toes or suffer bottlenecks along the route. Only in the popular "pacer-groups" of the 4-hour runners does the pack get rather tight in the first half. Anyone who is set on running 3:55 hours or faster will find they have plenty of space around themselves.

Since 2013 the Marathon Fair and the start line have been in the grounds of the Congress Center again and that has been a very good thing for the marathon. Previously the event had been, so to speak, "homeless," starting and finishing in places with no particular charm. But the Congress Center, where the start and finish now take place, have become the ideal meeting place where spectators and all those involved in the event can gather together during the marathon weekend, the site having the advantage of being easily reachable from all directions.

What is so special?
With a population of over 1.7 million inhabitants, Hamburg is an economic, cultural and international crossroads and a popular destination. Naturally it has the typical atmosphere of a major

port, described in numerous folk songs and sea shanties that resonated in the fish market but are still nostalgically romanticized today. It also has the sophisticated atmosphere of the rebuilt warehouse area HafenCity with its chic Marco Polo and Magellan terraces. Opposite is the Elbe Philharmonic Hall with a now completed facade that further enhances Hamburg's image while the city, architects and building companies continue to argue about the spiraling costs of the building. There are the magnificent villas of prosperous merchants round the Aussenalster (the Outer Alster Lake) and in the Blankenese

quarter, parts of which the marathon runners will discover. Another well-preserved cliché comes to life in the red-light district of St. Pauli and the Reeperbahn.

The route

The start of the marathon route or the sightseeing tour of the city begins at the exhibition halls of the Congress Center. Well, they should not be overrated; they are just exhibition halls with all the architectural charm that that implies. The route then passes by the Elbe, past the city's landmarks and along the Alster Lake.

Overall the Hamburg Marathon route is assessed as a fast course and attractions such as the Palace of Justice (top) are hardly noticed by the elite runners as they cover the ground (bottom).

The runners have a fine tour of the city, seeing all the highlights. A particular crowd-puller is the St. Pauli quayside (bottom) where the runners are seen in front of the magnificent backdrop of the harbor.

The first station is the Reeperbahn, in travel brochures often called Hamburg's "Sinful Mile" because of its red-light establishments. But since 2012 the Reeperbahn has acquired a much greater attraction: the dancing towers at the eastern end. These leaning towers are a real eye-catcher and an indication of how the streets will develop in the future; gentrification is in full swing in St. Pauli.

But even early in the morning, shortly after 9 o'clock, the Reeperbahn is open for business. As some runners start the first mile of the race full of confidence, the windows of the "horizontal profession" will be open in the buildings on the right side and occasionally the runners will hear some ambiguous remarks. Perhaps it is better to look at the theaters and restaurants on the left.

Soon the runners will pass the famous Davidwache, a police station that is widely recognized from its many appearances in movies and on television. Small as it is, in the last years it handled 15,695 complaints and 1,250 cases of fraud, mostly credit card fraud by prostitutes. By now many of the runners will be making the mistake of running too fast. A couple of hundred yards further on, Beatles-Platz is to the right. It was here that the Beatles played their first gig in Hamburg, celebrated by these sculptures of the musicians, cast in aluminum. There are five sculptures because in their early years the band had five members.

Immediately behind is "Susis-Show-Bar" and the junction with the "Grosse Freiheit," the entrance to the red-light district. The runners continue on the route that takes them towards Altona. The scenery is changing much faster than one can imagine. The route starts being lined with dense groups of spectators and music bands playing to cheer on the runners. Hamburg is already wide awake at 9 o'clock on this Sunday morning. After some 2.5 miles (6 km), the runners turn off from Bernadottestrasse into Halbmondsweg, the westernmost point of the route; 220 yards (200 m) later the route bends sharply to the left onto the magnificent Elbchaussee. The Elbe remains on the right of the route for the next 5 miles (8 km). At the 6.83 mile (11 km) mark, the port of Hamburg with its giant container cranes, busy even on Sundays, comes into view.

Perhaps one of these containers will be unloading running shoes? If the customs are quick, by Tuesday they will be on the shelves in Hamburg's fashionable shops. But every year about two million fake trainers which break trademark laws are discovered in containers like these by the Hamburg customs officers; all these fake trainers are immediately destroyed.

The view of the port along the Elbchaussee is frequently interrupted by magnificent rhododendrons of all colors which thrive in North Geremany's climate and soil. Often they are in full bloom during the marathon.

Party at the Klosterstern

The runners are greeted with enthusiasm by the spectators on the jetties in St. Pauli, a bit like they were a long awaited ship returning to its home port. Indeed, there is the atmosphere of a real port about this place, with the proud three-masted sailing ship Rickmer Rickmers moored to the quay. Soon the Elbe Philharmonic Hall and the red brick buildings of the warehouse district come into view before the route dives into the Wallring tunnel at the main station towards the Ballindamm. After the complete renovation of the Jungfernstieg promenade, the Inner Alster Lake has become a magnet for visitors, and not only during the marathon. The cafés and shops of the Jungfernstieg attract a lot of tourists and it is here that the numerous sightseeing boat excursions on the Alster and its branches start.

The runners may not have time to stop and look around, but the view from the handsome Lombardsbrücke, which is crossed in an eastward direction, is at least as beautiful as the Jungfernstieg itself. It divides the Outer and Inner Alster Lakes.

The second half of the race takes place along the east bank of the Alster where the locals have been gathering for a while along the road to cheer on the runners. Enthusiastic spectators line the route everywhere: on the Sierichstrasse, on the Südring, on the Überseering and in Alsterdorf. It is estimated that there are 600,000 spectators, most of them gathered along the second half of the route, so the runners are carried along by the cheering crowds towards the finish across the Klosterstern, the Aussenalster and Rotherbaum. In fact, an actual red carpet is rolled out at the finish line. There the runners can unreservedly let themselves to be treated like heroes.

"After a Marathon you think: 'If I can do this I can do anything.'"
Grete Waitz

INFORMATION

DATE End of April/Early May

PARTICIPANTS About 11,000 starters

CHARACTER OF THE ROUTE The premiere in 1986 was a bombshell: there were 8,309 participants on the starting line, more than ever before at a marathon premiere. Over half a million spectators lined the route. Many runners say that Hamburg has the best marathon atmosphere in Germany. The fast route is famous throughout the world.

ENTRY FEE From $80 (£47)

THE CITY The marathon circuit is an excellent tour of the major places of interest in the Hanseatic city. As a result the runners will be able to experience the colorful mix in the old city districts, along the Elbe and by the Alster Lakea as well as numerous tourist sites.

TIP FOR RUNNERS Runners should definitely treat themselves to a sightseeing run round the the Inner and Outer Alster Lake. From the northern shore of the Outer Alster Lake, you can see the Atlantic (this is the name of the hotel on the southern shore). The banks of the Elbe and the port districthave a completely different feel. In the Altona district runners will even be able to enjoy hill runs.

CONTACT DETAILS
Hamburg-Marathon
Carl-Cohn-Straße 71
22297 Hamburg
Germany
Tel.: +49/1805/77 17 60
E-Mail: office@marathonhamburg.de
Internet: www.haspa-marathon-hamburg.de

Summer

Marathon runners are not keen on hot weather but they love warm weather. Running carefree lightly clad makes the runner's heat beat faster. The long hours of sunshine invite one to run whatever the time. The summer vacation is perfect for planning a marathon trip whether in the United States or Europe or—a little tip for the runners—in the southern hemisphere, because it is winter there.

Runners in the SwissAlpine K42 Marathon in Davos, Switzerland.

Prague Experience: The old town is at the center of the Marathon route (top and center). In the course of the event the Vltava River is crossed several times (bottom).

Prague Marathon

With Dvořák at the start

The Prague Marathon shows the runners what the city has to offer. The route along the Vltava avoids the steep climbs on the right and left sides of the river.

It already feels very festive when the marathon starts to the sound of Antonin Dvorak's music in the Old Town Square. And those who still have images at the back of their mind of the 1989 Velvet Revolution will feel a slight shiver down the spine. Much has been achieved in the Czech Republic since and yet memories of life under socialist rule are still raw—this is quite obvious when you speak to the locals—and the traces are visible. There was some supportive help but not enough. There are gentrified old buildings in the picturesque old town but these are punctuated by the occasional crumbling facade or empty house.

But of course it is the ancient patina of the old town that gives this famous city on the Vltava its charm. Prague is often described as the "golden city," the "Paris of the East" or the "City with the Hundred Towers." The marathon runners will be quite aware of these sights even if they only see most of them from afar, such as the famous Prague Castle on the Hradschin dominating the old town. Most runners are relieved that this steep hill has not been included in the marathon route. Instead it runs through the historic center, through the heart of the medieval city and along the Vltava. The high point of the route is undoubtedly the crossing of the Charles Bridge, said by many to be the most beautiful Gothic bridge in the world. In fact, before or after the marathon, runners should take the time to go and admire the magnificent sculptures on the bridge piers.

An international field

The historic bridge is the second of eight bridges in the marathon and it is only 1.24 miles (2 km) from the start. So the runners are still concentrating on the cobblestones, the main pack is still tight and adrenalin levels are high. But after 1.86 miles (3 km) the marathon leaves the city along the wide riverside road and the pack starts to stretch out. The course continues to the mark at 4.97 miles (8 km) when the runners cross the Vltava again on the eastern turning-point. The runners now have a beautiful view of the vast extent of the Vltava wetlands and the wide sweep of the Vltava round the old town.

Prague is built on seven hills—hence the frequent comparison with Rome. The runners can see this but they do not feel it since the route is flat apart from the bridge crossings and underpasses. The number of different countries involved in the marathon is extraordinary. In recent years the organizers have recorded over 90 nationalities and half the participants come from abroad: a clear sign of Prague's increasing attraction as a tourist destination. Participants include many French, Italians, Germans, English and American runners.

A golf label for the "Golden City"

The Prague events are well attended: organizationally the Prague marathon is part of a whole series of running events in the Czech Republic that have deliberately developed an international dimension, supported by an excellent international infra-structure. The International Amateur Athletic Association has awarded the marathon its gold label.

After a further 7.45 miles (12 km) the runners reach the finish line in the Old Town Square where they are greeted by more cheering spectators. The runners will feel that all the terrible cobblestones are a thing of the past and they will prefer to remember the many bands who have spured them on at regular intervals with their music.

At night the center throbs with revelers who only return home in the small hours of the morning: Prague is of course famous for its nightlife and club culture. There are many reasons to visit the city and the marathon is a particularly good one.

"Why should I train slowly? I know how to do that. I want to learn how to run fast! "

Emil Zátopek

INFORMATION

DATE May

PARTICIPANTS About 9,500 starters

CHARACTER OF THE ROUTE A flat city circuit. For runners the bridges and the stretches with cobblestones are the greatest challenge. In addition, in Prague it can get very hot and sunny in May which is why there are numerous refreshment posts. At the finish Czech beer is served. There are also shorter runs, interesting for those visiting the city accompanying serious runners, as well as an original separate event, Walk with Dogs.

ENTRY FEE From $105 (£62)

THE CITY Prague is quite rightly considered one of the up-and-coming European capitals. The tourist places of interest and attractions range from the medieval town center to modern art. It is possible to stay in international hotels but there are also in private guesthouses for smaller budgets.

TIP FOR RUNNERS You should definitely indulge in an early morning run along the banks of the Vltava as far as the the Charles Bridge. Normally overrun with tourists, the bridge is still empty at that time. The river banks and meadows are beautiful running tracks.

CONTACT DETAILS
International Office
Prague International Marathon
Zahoranskeho 3
120 00 Praha 2
Czech Republic
E-Mail: info@praguemarathon.com
Internet: www.praguemarathon.co

Masonry. The Great Wall is a stunning experience and the runners are often short of breath. Many parts of the route have to be climbed at a walking pace.

Great Wall Marathon

When runners experience the Wall

Running along a section of the Great Wall in China is a incredible experience. But running a whole marathon here is also unique achievement. The runners will have a long-lasting impression of this extraordinary construction, which is on the list of the UNESCO-World Heritage sites.

The Great Wall of China is one of the oldest and most impressive constructions in the world. The building of this protective wall was started in the 5th century BC and it winds its way across 5,500.4 miles (8,851.8 km), according to the measurements of the Chinese government. Standing on one of the scenic viewpoints on the wall, one can hardly imagine the terrible conditions under which the workers who built this bastion worked or the pressure that was applied to them. The longest wall in the world symbolized national power, identity and pride—and it still does so today.

Today there are several sports events involving the Great Wall. In recent years there have been two marathons a year which have proved extremely popular, one in May and one in September. The route of the May marathon is mainly alongside the wall, with about 2.5 miles (4 km) on the wall itself. In the selected route there are 5,164 steps to be climbed This is a strenuous challenge, because of

course the steps do not meet today's architectural standards but they all differ in shape, height length and size.

Long finishing times

The marathon is held in the Chinese province of Tianjin while the start and finish are in Huangyaguan which can be reached from Beijing after a coach trip of 93 miles (10 km). The marathon starts early, at about 7.30 a.m., to avoid the increasing heat and humidity during the day. Some runners will find it a real torture if they are not sufficiently prepared. Jochen Temsch, who in 2010 struggled on the wall as a running journalist, wrote: "Some were swearing, half in jest. Many were laughing insanely. Others were fighting free-style against the threat of cramps in their legs: they would hobble down the steps backwards or try to walk up sideways."

The surrounding landscape is very mountainous. And the steps are treacherous; some of them knee-high, then very low again, sometimes wide and sprawling, then narrow, and always with just a thin steel cable to protect the runners from the abyss. Many uphill and downhill stretches climb or descend about 1,000 ft (300 m) at a time. It is not surprising that participants claim it is the most difficult marathon there is, although the nature trails and dirt roads that run beside the walls are not too bad. There are also some rough tracks.

Communicating with gestures

The second marathon event really deserves its name: the Chinese Great Wall Marathon, organized by Wichart Hölscher from Munich, takes place entirely on the wall itself, making it one of the most spectacular marathon events in the world. Hölscher himself warns that "the route is not easy!" Runners have to contend with an elevation gain of about 5,600 ft (1,700 m). Fortunately there is no time limit.

The marathon is run on a less-known part of the wall, Jinshanling, about 75 miles (120 km) to the north of Beijing. The running conditions are good, the air clear and rather dry and the sky is blue. There are participants from over 50 countries but because the route involves a turning-point on the wall, the number of people taking part is limited to 500. Economically, it is very beneficial for this somewhat deprived region.

Runners will also enjoy another side of China, the countryside. There excited children run along with you for a few steps, handing out flowers, and bananas. They overcome the language problem by communicating with gestures rather than words.

"Even a long run begins with a single step."
Confucius

INFORMATION

DATE May

PARTICIPANTS About 2,000 starters

CHARACTER OF THE ROUTE Very hilly across gravel paths and country roads, it is a demanding event. The route combines nature, culture and a sporting experience. Anyone who wants to get to know something about China will find this a concentrated and fascinating way of doing so.

ENTRY FEE From $2,800 (£1,650) for a 6-day trip including Marathon

THE REGION The Tianjin region is a picturesque destination that is very much worth visiting. The Chinese themselves and the marathon organisers are well aware of this and the province can now be reached quite easily and quickly from Beijing. The advantage of the second date in September is that it uses a part of the wall that is less visited by tourists, so the runners are more on their own.

TIP FOR RUNNERS The number of places in both events is strictly limited so registration in July of the previous year is recommended. The courses are demanding and a good level of training is essential.

CONTACT DETAILS

Registration is through a tour operator.

The Rennsteig Marathon is extremely traditional and this is really appreciated. More than half the participants have run in it before and many of them come back every year.

Rennsteig Marathon

Tradition-bound

Formerly in the German Democratic Republic, the Rennsteig marathon is not so well known as the big-city marathons. But as far as atmosphere is concerned, it can certainly hold its own.

Everyone calls this marathon the Rennsteig Race and by this they mean the GutsMuths-Rennsteig race. It is a classic on the running scene with many die-hard fans who keep coming back again and again. These repeat runners represent over 50 percent of the participants, and it is estimated that by now more than 800 runners have taken part in the Rennsteig race more than 25 times. One of the co-founders, Hans-Joachim Römhild had already run it 40 times so far, only missing one year since he started. Another regular, Roland Winkler, took part for the first time in 1975 and he won the Ultramarathon of about 45 miles (73 km) in 1976. He plans to continue running in the race until at least 2024, which will be his 50th time.

Where does this euphoric loyalty come from? For a start, there is the beauty of the route: the Rennsteig is an ancient path running along a ridge through the Thuringian Forest, a low mountain range forming a magnificent landscape. And then there is tradition. The marathon has taken place since the 1970s and it soon became the biggest mass sport event in the then German

Democratic Republic. It has successfully resisted all conflicts of interest and attempts to exploit it. Today it has acquired a cult status.

The event is named after Christoph GutsMuths a sports educator born in 1759. He is recognized as the founder of gymnastics and actively promoted the concept of physical training for young people.

A relaxed atmosphere

Here the marathon distance is longer than the standard, being 27 miles (43.5 km) long, an example of Thuringian individuality. Starting in Neuhaus, the marathon is just one of several events, involving 15,000 runners altogether. Over 2,000 runners take part in the 44.8 mile (72.2 km) Ultramarathon, which starts in Eisenach. This route is also a point-point race, with climbs amounting to 2,090 ft (637 m) and descents to 2,316 ft (439 m). The finish for all the races is on the sports ground in Schmiedefeld. Available along the route is Schwarzbier, a black beer that is a specialty of the region.

As early as 1971 and 1972 a few fearless "comrades in sport" set off on test runs on the then accessible part of the Rennsteig. The first such run was from Eisenach to Masserberg, a distance of 55.7 miles (89.65 km). This was completed by four runners, including the founder Hans-Georg Kremer, who later became responsible for the overall organization.

East and West together

The routes varied. In 1974 twelve runners competed over 62.1 miles (100 km) and in 1975 a first invitation to register was handed out to students and sports associations in the German Democratic Republic. In 1976 the Star Run concept was applied, with different starting points for the various distances, but with a common finishing point at Schmiedefeld. In 1977 the marathon distance was run for the first time, in parallel with the Ultramarathon, and a total of 4,454 runners took part. Eighteen clubs were involved in the organization and thirteen of them still involved today. In 1979 the event took another step forward: the Rennsteiglauf event was advertised publicly and 4,604 participants crossed the finishing line.

The year 1990 was an important one, being the year of German reunification. On April 28, the borders dividing Germany were officially opened. So on May 19, 1990, the runners lining up to take part in the Rennsteiglauf included 600 participants from the former Federal Republic of Germany.

Open to a wide range of categories, this event pursues the ideals that were championed by Gutsmuths: "For health and vitality, take part in sport!"

"I love climbs! I see the challenge and the destination, and I am electrified to accomplish it."
Amby Burfoot

INFORMATION

DATE May

PARTICIPANTS About 3,200 starters

CHARACTER OF THE ROUTE It doesn't matter who you are: children, ultra runners, ramblers, amateurs and handicapped sportsmen are all welcome here and this hill climb race is like a big family get-together. The organizers describe it as Europe's biggest cross-country run, so anyone who loves running in the countryside will be at home here. The down-to-earth approach is part of its appeal. Instead of a "pasta party" the evening before there is a "dumpling party." The run is definitely a cult event.

ENTRY FEE From $56 (£32)

THE REGION The Thuringian Forest is a paradise for ramblers and athletes. Here runners will find her a wide network of well sign-posted tracks. The Rennsteig or ridge walk is over 100 miles (160 km) and can be run in several stages. The transport of your luggage can be arranged.

TIP FOR RUNNERS The Thuringian Forest is a rewarding destination for nature-loving runners and anyone who is interested in beautiful scenery throughout the year—except in winter when the snow means that it is taken over by skiers.

CONTACT DETAILS
Rennsteiglauf GmbH
Schmückestraße 74
98711 Schmiedefeld a. R.
Germany
Tel.: +49/36782/612 37
E-Mail: info@rennsteiglauf.de
Internet: www.rennsteiglauf.de

Not sports crazy, but extremely enthusiastic: the Swedes have a very positive attitude as they run through their capital.

Stockholm Marathon

Running through the floating capital

Anyone who does not yet know the city of Stockholm should run the marathon. There is no better way of getting an impression of the Swedish capital in such a short time.

It is true, there is one perspective that marathon runners will not be able to enjoy: the view from the sea. It is self-evident that water is as much a part of Stockholm as the flat-pack furniture retailer IKEA. The description of the route gives pause for thought: it is run in two laps, meaning that participants run over much of the same circuit twice. From the competitor's point of view it has advantages too, since the route will become familiar: in the second lap the runner will recognize many of the streets, the buildings and large public open spaces, landmarks that have already been passed before. This is a great boost to the self-confidence. There are also definite advantages for the organizer: the length of streets to be closed off is reduced, as is the number of refreshment points, stewards and route markings. It is also more entertaining for many of the spectators who will be able to see the runners more often.

Sports-minded Sweden

Sweden has a very good sports atmosphere. "Admittedly, the Swedes may not be sports-crazy,

they too reticent for that, but they are reasonably enthusiastic about it and enjoy taking part in it," says Hans Lodin, the editor of the Swedish edition of the magazine Runner's World. In Sweden, anyone who has taken part in the Swedish Classic Circuit or in at least in one of its four race disciplines is much admired. The competition consists of four endurance disciplines: the Lidingöloppet cross-country run, cross-country skiing, open-air swimming and cycling. At the same time, there are also long and ultra-long distance races, for example the "Vasoloppet," a cross-country ski race over 56 miles (90 km) in classic style. This is the biggest sports event in Sweden and its television viewing figures are as high as those for World Cup football matches or the Olympic Games. Here too we see the Swedes' enthusiasm for national sports events.

As Hans Lodin explains: "The Swedes are a very sporting people. Any foreigner who completes the Vasaloppet race can be sure of receiving the highest recognition." This sporting attitude is also evident in the Stockholm Marathon, a fact reflected in the large

number of spectators and also in the high level of support.

A retro look and a later start

Many spectators come and watch the marathon dressed in historic costume, a tribute to the 1912 Stockholm Olympics Marathon. The tradition for spectators to dress up started with the Jubilee Marathon which took place in 2012 in parallel with the classic Stockholm Marathon. This tradition ties in perfectly with the setting because the start of the race takes place on the Lidingövägen, outside the historic stadium built for the 1912 Olympic Games.

Then the first lap starts. With a length of 10.31 miles (16.6 km), it is much shorter than the second one which is 15.91 miles (25.6 km). There are only two curves in the first mile or so (2 km) and it is slightly downhill, making it is very difficult not to run too fast. But for those starting at the rear, the field is still so crowded together that the speed is automatically slowed down. Another interesting feature about the Stockholm marathon is that it starts at 11.30 a.m., much later than most of the other big-city marathons. Some runners think this is a good thing and others not; it depends on the individual.

The route of the Marathon takes the runners right to the heart of the Swedish capital. Here they are running through Gamla Stan, the Old Town.

After 2.5 miles (4 km) the runners reach the water as they approach the magnificent Strandvägen boulevard. The special relationship that the Swedes have with water is understandable when one realizes that the country has many more miles of coastline than its borders with other countries. Stockholm itself is built on 14 islands so it is both surrounded and traversed by water: in other words, it is a floating capital. And as you approach Stockholm from the sea you pass through its famous archipelago of 24,000 islands. The affinity with water and water sports is therefore no coincidence. There are many tempting speedboat excursions carrying visitors from the center of Stockholm to this unique labyrinth of islands.

But the opening section of the marathon is through the Stockholm city centre. All hell breaks loose on the Kungsträdgården, the former kitchen garden of the medieval court. Here there are crowds cheering on the runners as music plays. Here too is the first of the many refreshment points, placed at short intervals along the marathon route. In years when the weather is cool their number may seem surprising, but when it is hot, the runners are happy to have so many. By May the weather can be very hot during the day although the air remains relatively cool. Nevertheless it is often warm enough to slow the runners down. This is why each section of the marathon must be approached calmly.

Now the runners reach Gamla Stan, the celebrated Old Town. On the right is the Royal Palace and the runners then continue past a row of historic

houses. Off Skeppsholmen island on the opposite bank, the runners will see the Chapman sailing ship that is moored there. Adventurous and price-conscious tourists should bear it in mind because the magnificent, beautifully restored sailing ship is now a youth hostel within walking distance of the city centre. At this point the runners will have covered the first 3.1 miles (5 km) while passing on the second lap they will have run 18.6 miles (30 km). Just round the corner is the next highlight so far as the spectators are concerned. At the end of Skeppsbron island is the lock where the Baltic Sea meets Lake Mälaren—and here drinks are available.

A rewarding climb

The route continues to follow through the Södermalm quarter from which the runners can already see the Västerbron bridge looming ahead of them. Many runners fear the climb, the only serious one in the entire marathon. The bridge is 100 ft (30 m) high and sometimes a fierce wind can blow here. In compensation, the runners have a wonderful view of Stockholm and its mosaic of ancient and modern

The Marathon gives many impressions of Stockholm (top). An absolute highlight is the finish in the old Olympic Stadium (above right), full of spectators watching the runners arrive (bottom).

buildings. The view from the Västerbron bridge is well-guarded secret and not many tourists discover it!

The route now takes the runners through the Kungsholmen district, past the City Hall and through the Norrmalm district on the way to the city centre where the Central Station is situated. The route then slopes down gently towards the mark at 9.3 miles (15 km), so the end of the first lap will soon be reached. The Olympic Stadium is on the left again but the route continues straight ahead, and it is at this point that the pressure of the marathon starts for real: now the runners really need to be fit. The route is the same as the first lap as far as the Ozxenstierngatan boulevard but it then turns left into the diplomatic district. The highlight of the second lap is the detour through Djurgården, the green lungs of the city, a wonderful green area with a leisure park and several museums. Here the runners can admire the old trees, wild meadows and well-kept green spaces of the former animal garden. Rejoining the route at the Strandvägen boulevard, already described in the first lap, the runners will be aware how far it is from here since they are covering the same ground again. They are already familiar with Gamla Stan, the Old Town, and being by now exhausted the Västerbron Bridge will feel even higher to them than the first time round.

But the absolute highlight of the marathon is the last mile, finishing inside the old Olympic stadium, crowded with marathon fans who create a fantastic atmosphere.

"Every runner knows that running is more than putting one foot in front of the other. It's a lifestyle."

Joan Benoit Samuelson

INFORMATION

DATE May

PARTICIPANTS About 21,500 starters

CHARACTER OF THE ROUTE This Marathon consists of a scenic two-lap course through Stockholm's inner center with the finish in the old Olympic stadium, built in 1912. The route takes the runners past the Royal Palace, the Town Hall, the Royal Opera House and the Parliament. There are large numbers of spectators, many bands and an international field of runners, about a third of them from abroad. The route is not too demanding in spite of having an elevation gain of 1,300 ft (400 m).

ENTRY FEE From $225 (£95)

THE CITY In May the sun does not set until 10 p.m. in Stockholm—the day is very long. And there is much to see. History and modernism go hand in hand here, so a tour of the city and an outing to the Stockholm archipelago are both highly recommended.

TIP FOR RUNNERS A must for all Stockholm visitors is a training tour through the Djurgården, one of the most beautiful city parks in Europe and a popular stamping ground for runners.

CONTACT DETAILS

Stockholm Marathon
15124
16715 Bromma
Sweden
Tel.: +46/8/54 56 64 40
Fax: +46/8/664 38 22
E-Mail: info@marathon.se
Internet: www.stockholmmarathon.se

The desire to run a marathon comes from the pleasure of running.

Marathon training
Planning for success: training for the first marathon

"Life itself is a marathon," said the actor Dieter Hallervorden in playing the role of Paul Averhoff in the movie His last Race. Hallervorden plays the part of a former Olympic winner in a marathon race that he compares to his own life: as in life, in a marathon nothing comes for nothing. It just does not work like that. It demands effort, planning, hardship and focus. The movie is quite right and anyone who wants to run a marathon must be aware

of this. It should be seen as a carefully planned project, one's own "Marathon project."

To begin with, it is important to set oneself a realistic target. Then one should devise a realistic plan to achieve this target. It is only then that you can convert this plan into a series of concrete stags. "And at the end is victory, absolutely certain victory," according to the character Paul Averhoff. This is no

exaggeration: there are few events in a person's life from which so much self-confidence, pride and joy can be gained with such a long-lasting effect as completing a marathon.

A planning game
Anyone setting a challenging goal—and running a marathon is undoubtedly a major challenge—must ask him or herself a few

questions before starting planning. As far as the running aspect itself is concerned, the questions are as follows:

1. Do I feel I am healthy enough and physically able to prepare myself for a marathon and to run it?
2. Am I mentally able to rise to the challenge of running a marathon?
3. Can I reconcile this project with my home life, my social life and my work? That is, without neglecting my partner, family and friends or work too much?
4. It is a big project. What can I compare it with, what other projects have or have had that kind of importance for me? And where does running stand as far as I am concerned?
5. Why do I want to run a marathon?

Overall objectives

The goals you set for a marathon will always depends on your current training condition. Are you a novice runner ? Or a novice marathon runner who already runs regularly and is now planning a first marathon? Or an experienced runner aiming for a new best time? Or are you a top runner who is keen to secure a good placing as well as making a good time?

Sit down at a table and picture that whole tabletop as an image of your marathon plan. The left edge of the table is the start of your preparation while the right edge represents the finish line of the marathon. As a novice there is a time span of two or even three years of running experience ahead of you before you reach the right edge of the table, that is, before you can run your first marathon. If you are already an experienced runner the time will be shorter, as if you were starting nearer the middle of the tabletop.

There are cases of marathon runners who started from scratch and completed their preparation in a much shorter time. But most people who have not prepared themselves over a long enough period do not run any more afterwards, or they give up on the way as a result of injury.

With very few exceptions, most people who run a marathon focus on a healthy lifestyle, physical health, fitness and mental wellbeing. And this should also the overall objective in planning a marathon. It means that the marathon project will have to be canceled in the case of an injury lasting longer than two weeks or if the preparation turns out to be too cumbersome.

Setting concrete objectives

As in all project planning, when deciding to run a marathon, the reasons for doing so must be defined. The overall objective for most runners is health in the long term—that is, continuing indefinitely after the marathon. There are three decisive factors that will affect the impending planning:

1. What is your current fitness and training situation?
2. How much time is available for training? Here professional and personal aspects must be taken into consideration, because training for a marathon will inevitably take up some of your free time.
3. What kind of result are you aiming for? Here there are

Training for running is entierly up to you.

Training together. A couple can talk while running, while maintaing the correct training pace.

"minimum" goals such as simply crossing the finish line, while the time you take to finish it does not matter. Then there are "maximum" goals such as aiming to finish within a particular time, for instance "under 4 hours" or "improving one's personal best time."

Therefore training and training objectives must be adapted to the individual. The target time to be achieved will depend on your running experience and your performance level at the start of the training period. This is the advantage of running: an experienced trainer will be able to draw up a personalized training plan for you. This make the planning easier to organize and it will also be healthier, since it will take account of your personal situation. You can be confident that you are preparing yourself in the best way. The effects of training will not happen overnight but will be very aware of them when running. The most important effects of training are:

- The cardiovascular system is strengthened. The lungs function better, the blood vessels expand, the heart becomes stronger and it can pump more blood.
- The muscles become stronger.
- The body goes through a learning process, learning how to burn energy more efficiently and drawing on the body's fat reserves earlier and more effectively—a process known as fat-burning.

Training plan

For a trained runner who is already running 19 miles (30 km) a week, the immediate preparation phase for a marathon is usually twelve weeks—possibly less but seldom more. The plan has a structured, recurrent build-up. The extent, speed and frequency of training vary. When training for a first marathon, quantity is a major consideration, that is the amount of time spent running. This does not simply mean "more is better" but the duration and intensity should follow the training plan strictly. At

Training together is motivating and helps you evaluate your own performance better.

Tempo training. Anyone who runs quickly in training can do the same in competition.

The perfect arm position: slightly bent.

this level the running speed and pulse of the runner are fairly low.

Principles of training

Regularity: The main training objective is simple. The body must adapt to the stress of running so that running a marathon is possible at the end of the preparation phase. This is why the level of training is systematically raised and the number of training days per week increases. Starting with three days a week, it may go up to six days a week, depending on the marathon objective. But the important thing is that this all happens very slowly, with no abrupt increases in duration or frequency. As a rule of thumb, the duration and frequency should not increase by more than 15 percent a week. This is especially important in the case of the weekly long run, which must not be increased by more than 15 minutes each time.

Here is an example. In the case of a novice marathon runner training four times a week, three of the runs must not exceed one hour but the

WEEK 1

Tues. 30 min faster ER
Thur. 35 min fartlek (changing pace at will)
Sat. 20–30 min steady ER
Sun. 90 min easy ER, incl. 3 min breaks after 30 and 60 min
↺ **Total: 3:00 h**

WEEK 2

Tues. 30 min steady ER
Thur. 40 min faster ER
Sat. 20 min steady ER, then 5 increases
Sun. 6 miles (10 km) competition or hard test run over the same distance 10 min out and back
Total: 2:30 h

WEEK 3

Tues. 35 min easy ER
Thur. 40 min fartlek (changing pace at will)
Sun. 105 min easy ER, incl. 3 min break after 30, 60, 90 min
↺ **Total: 3:00 h**

WEEK 4

Tues. 35 min faster ER
Thur. 35 min fartlek (changing pace at will)
Sun. 120 min easy ER, incl. 3 min break at 30 min
Total: 3:10 h

WEEK 5

Tues. 30 min faster ER
Thur. 20 min easy ER, then 5 increases
Sun. Half-marathon competition (every 3 miles ,5 km, a 1 minute catering stop)
↺ **Total: 3:00 h**

WEEK 6

Tues. 20 min easy ER
Thur. 25 min fartlek (changing pace at will)
Sun. 135 min easy ER, incl. 3 min break at 30 min
↺ **Total: 3:00 h**

WEEK 7

Tues. 20 min steady ER
Thur. 20 min fartlek (changing pace at will)
Sat. 150 min easy ER, incl. 3 min break at 30 min
↺ **Total: 3:10 h**

WEEK 8

Tues. 20 min steady ER
Thur. 20 min fartlek (changing pace at will)
Sat. 150 min easy ER, incl. 3 min break at 30 min
↺ **Total: 3:10 h**

WEEK 9

Tues. 30 min faster ER
Thur. 30 min fartlek (changing pace at will)
Sat. 30 min faster ER
Sun. 30 min at marathon race speed
↺ **Total: 2:00 h**

WEEK 10

Wed. 30 min faster ER, then 3 increases
Sat. 15 min easy ER, then 3 increases
Sun. Marathon

TRAINING PLAN FOR A MARATHON IN 3:59:59

WEEK 1 ⮂ **about 31–34 miles (50–55 km)**

Mon. 60 min faster ER

Tues. Rest day

Wed. 60 min fartlek (changing pace at will)

Thur. Rest day

Fr 60 min faster ER

Sat. Rest day

Sun. 14 miles (22 km) easy ER (every 3 miles, 5 km, a short break for a drink)

WEEK 2 ⮂ **about 28 miles (45 km)**

Mon. Rest day

Tues. 50 min faster ER

Wed. 60 min fartlek (changing pace at will)

Thur. Rest day

Fr 50 min faster ER

Sat. Rest day

Sun. 6 miles (10 km) competition, with 1 mile (2 km) each out and back

WEEK 3 ⮂ **about 34–37 miles (55–60 km)**

Mon. Rest day

Tues. 60 min easy ER

Wed. Rest day

Thur. 50 min faster ER, then 5 sprints over 328 ft (100 m)

Fr 60 min fartlek (changing pace at will)

Sat. Rest day

Sun. 15.5 miles (25 km) easy ER (every 3 miles, 5 km, a short break for a drink)

WEEK 4 ⮂ **about 37 miles (60 km)**

Mon. Rest day

Tues. 60 min faster ER

Wed. Rest day

Thur. 1 mile (2 km) run up, 5 miles (8 km) at planned marathon race pace, 1 mile (2 km) run down

Fr 50 min faster ER

Sat. Rest day

Sun. 15–17 miles (25–28 km) easy ER (every 3 miles, 5 km, a short break for a drink)

WEEK 5 ⮂ **about 37 miles (60 km)**

Mon. Rest day

Tues. 60 min faster ER

Wed. Rest day

Thur. 1 mile (2 km) run up, 26 x 2,625 (8 x 800 m) in 3:59 min (jogging break 3 min), 1 mile (2 km) run down

Fr 60 min faster ER

Sat. Rest day

Sun. 17 miles (28 km) easy ER (every 3 miles, 5 km, a short break for a drink)

WEEK 6 ⮂ **about 40 miles (65 km)**

Mon. Rest day

Tues. 40 min faster ER

Wed. 1 mile (2 km) run up, 6 miles (10 km) at planned marathon race pace, 1 mile (2 km) run down

Thur. Rest day

Fr 60 min faster ER

Sat. Rest day

Sun. 19 miles (30 km) easy ER (every 3 miles, 5 km, a short break for a drink)

WEEK 7 ⮂ **about 28 miles (45 km)**

Mon. Rest day

Tues. 40 min faster ER

Wed. 1 mile (2 km) run up, 4 x 4 min faster ER (jogging break 2 min), 1 mile (2 km) run down

Thur. Rest day

Fr 30 min easy ER, then 5 increases

Sat. Rest day

Sun. 6 miles (10 km) competition (or hard test run over same distance) with run up and run down)

WEEK 8 ⮂ **about 37–40 miles (60–65 km)**

Mon. Rest day

Tues. 50 min faster ER

Wed. 60 min faster ER

Thur. Rest day

Fr 60 min fartlek (changing pace at will)

Sat. Rest day

Sun. 20 miles (32 km) easy ER (every 3 miles, 5 km, a short break for a drink)

WEEK 9 ⮂ **about 40 miles (65 km)**

Mon. Rest day

Tues. 60 min faster ER

Wed. Rest day

Thur. 1 mile (2 km) run up, 5 x 5 min faster ER (jogging pause 4 min), 1 mile (2 km) run down

Fr 50 min faster ER

Sat. Rest day

Sun. 20 miles (32 km) easy ER (every 3 miles, 5 km, a short break for a drink)

WEEK 10 ⮂ **about 37 miles (60 km)**

Mon. Rest day

Tues. 1 mile (2 km) run up, pyramid run: 3 min, 6 min, 9 min, 6 min, 3 min faster ER (jogging pause 3 min, 5 min, 7 min, 5 min), 1 mile (2 km) run down

Wed. Rest day

Thur. 60 min faster ER

Fr 1 mile (2 km) run up, 6 miles (10 km) at planned marathon pace, 1 mile (2 km) run down

Sat. Rest day

Sun. 20 miles (32 km) easy ER (every 3 miles, 5 km, a short break for a drink)

WEEK 11 ⮂ **about 22 miles (35 km)**

Mon. Rest day

Tues. 40 min easy ER

Wed. 6 miles (10 km) fartlek (changing pace)

Thur. Rest day

Fr 60 min faster ER

Sat. Rest day

Sun. 30 min easy ER, 5 increases

WEEK 12

Mon. Rest day

Tues. 1 mile (2 km) run up, 3 miles (5 km) at planned marathon pace, 1 mile (2 km) run down

Wed. Rest day

Thur. 20 min easy ER, then 3 increases

Fr Rest day

Sat. 15 min easy ER, hen 3 increases

Sun. Marathon

long run, on the other hand, can last three hours.

Stress and recuperation: Each training session is followed by a rest period. This is an important ground rule in training. A long preparation run is followed by a correspondingly longer rest period. In order to complete the next long run without experiencing problems, the famous US trainer Jeff Galloway recommends allowing one day of rest for each mile run. Galloway advises all marathon runners—including top athletes—to take two days' rest a week.

Continuous intensification: When preparing for a marathon, the weekly distance is progressively increased. Runners who want to complete the marathon in less than four hours must reckon on a training schedule of at least 30 to 40 miles (50 to 60 km). In addition, there are other requirements which must be met, such as ideal body weight, perfect health and no injuries of any kind. The core training session in the preparation for a marathon is the

THE RIGHT SPEED

Explanation of the terms and abbreviations in the Training Plan

ER = Endurance run

JP = Jogging pause (pause between stress sessions)

Easy ER = heart rate about 70 or 75 percent of the maximum heart rate

Steady ER = heart rate about 75-80 percent of the maximum heart rate

Faster ER = pulse about 80-85 percent of the maximum heart rate

Threshold ER = heart rate about 85-88 percent of the maximum heart rate

fartlek = alternating speed over stretches of different lengths. Speed and duration of the stress are varied at will.

Racing speed = pace during competition under normal conditions

Intensification = running over a distance of 88 to 110 yards (80 to 100 m) with the pace progressively increasing from jogging to sprint.

TR = Timed runs (prepare with 10 minutes warm-up and end with 10 minutes warm-down)

EXAMPLE TRAINING PLAN FOR A "MARATHON UNDER 4 HOURS"

Anyone who completes a marathon in under 4 hours will usually end up in the first half of the field in most events. The goal is ambitious and it requires concentrated and planned training. Running expert Martin Grüning recommends a general training plan for the last twelve weeks before the marathon in addition to an individual training plan adapted to the particular objective (see page 72).

long run, where the duration is more important than the distance.

A training plan to finish the run

The first marathon is always an experiment. No one can anticipate what will happen during the race:

how the body will react, how it will function, whether muscle cramps will occur or whether the stomach will object. It is unpredictable. But it would be reckless and unhealthy to tackle a marathon without any special preparation. Training expert Martin Grüning, in his time one of the best marathon runners (best time 2:13:30 hours) and today one of the most experienced marathon trainers, has worked out a special training program for runners who want (or are able) to train as little as possible but who want to complete the marathon. This is the minimal marathon training plan (see page 71, "Training plan to finish"). Runners with enough running experience can organize their marathon preparations with this minimal training plan which takes three hours a week. It will not result in super-fast times but it will be enough to keep up.

Tempo runs or fartlek runs are good for training in a group.

San Francisco (top) is full of surprises.
one runner is wearing his dream girl's
veil (bottom) and another just before the
finish is dressed as a joker (center).

San Francisco Marathon
The Bridge in International Orange

The number 42 is a magical one for marathon runners, being
a marathon's length in kilometers. In San Francisco it has an
additional significance, being the number of hills in the urban
area. Runners will come to know these steep climbs personally.
This is both a warning and a promise.

San Francisco is one of the world's
most popular tourist destinations.
And the city's most distinctive feature,
the Golden Gate Bridge, is one of the
most famous structures in the United
States. It is crossed twice in the San
Francisco marathon, and this alone
is a good enough reason for many
runners to take part in it.

Visitors will find the city a perfect
example of American culture and at
the same time the most European of
all American cities. This is reflected in
many aspects of the city, including its
architecture, its culture and its politics.

Runners like in the Gold Rush
The marathon gives an excellent
overall impression of the city and
naturally it includes all the famous
tourist sights. The most famous of
them, the Golden Gate Bridge, is
reached after about 5 miles (8 km).
This suspension bridge takes its
name from the 19th-century Gold
Rush when the town suddenly grew
phenomenally. The bridge has great

symbolic importance but it also
invaluable in terms of road traffic.
For this reason the marathon starts
at 5.30 a.m. so that the bridge can
be opened to traffic again later in the
morning.

Even the start of the marathon
is incredibly beautiful. In these
first miles the route follows the
Embarcadero towards the famous
Fisherman's Wharf, including Pier
39: here the former fish market halls
and warehouses have now become
restaurants and shops attracting a
large number of tourists. The island
of Alacatraz, just off the coast and
famous for its notorious prison, keeps
coming back into view.

The route through Fort Mason
and Marina Green Drive is amazingly
beautiful and continues along the
shore enabling the runners to enjoy
the sound of the waves and the view
of the Golden Gate Bridge. With
a total length from abutment to
abutment of nearly 1.74 miles (2.8
km), the bridge spanning the Golden

Gate Strait feels even longer when you run across it. There are many marathons where the route crosses a number of bridges, such as those of Amsterdam, Venice or New York. But crossing the Golden Gate Bridge in running shoes is in a league of its own, given the elegance of the bridge and its magnificent setting.

For the photo album
Its color "International Orange" has been patented. It stands out beautifully against the morning and evening sky and it is not surprising that this gigantic, harmonious structure is the world's most photographed bridge.

After a U-turn at the northern viewpoint, the runners are rewarded with a panoramic view of San

Francisco. From a scenic point of view, the route continues along the Pacific coast overlooking the popular Baker Beach. The proximity of the Pacific Ocean with its cooling effect results in pleasant temperatures for running even though the marathon is held in the summer months.

The runners reach the halfway point in the marathon in the exquisitely designed Golden Gate Park, another demonstration of the way in which the San Francisco marathon combines varied picturesque scenery with a city atmosphere. The second half of the marathon is slightly easier and more urban, going through the Haight-Ashbury and Mission Bay districts. Encouraged by lively music, the finish is right next to Bay Bridge at the Ferry Building.

"Being an athlete must be something to do with consciousness, not with age, performance or placing."
Jeff Galloway

INFORMATION

DATE June/July

PARTICIPANTS About 15,000 starters

CHARACTER OF THE ROUTE The course is a varied one, embracing the city, its parks and greenery, the Pacific coast and naturally the Golden Gate Bridge that is a hill in itself, rising up at about 3 degrees to the center. The time limit is six hours and the start is very early in the morning, at 5.30 a.m. There are several other runs associated with the event, including two half-marathons and a double marathon.

ENTRY FEE From $110 (£65)

THE CITY San Francisco is a business and financial center that is also well-known as a liberal, open-minded city for individuals of all kinds, bohemians and hippies. It is an excellent starting point for trips to the West Coast, both north and south on Highway 1.

TIP FOR RUNNERS Nearby there is a perfect place for people who are looking for a quiet, scenic area to run in. It is reached by crossing the Golden Gate Bridge and running in the Golden Gate National Recreation Area Natural Park, along the coast with a unique view of the city and the sea. Another option is the parkland within the Presidio.

CONTACT DETAILS
RunSFM
PO Box 77148
San Francisco, CA 94107
United States
Tel.: +1/888/958 66 68
E-Mail: info@thesfmarathon.com
Internet: www.thesfmarathon.com

Big Five Marathon
Survival of the fittest

The "Big Five" safari area is so-called after the five famous rulers of the South African veldt: the lion, leopard, elephant, rhinoceros and buffalo. These wild animals are onlookers at the Big Five Marathon. The atmosphere is very peaceful, the greatest challenge being the actual marathon. It is a unique experience!

Running in the wilderness. Anyone who has only run city marathons or trained by running on asphalt will find a completely different experience here. Game wardens protect the runners from wild animals.

The countryside near the Limpopo River in northern South Africa is breathtakingly beautiful and a unique habitat for wild animals. Animals live freely here that in the rest of the world are seen only in zoos, behind thick rails and enclosed by a wide ditch. The Limpopo provincce has been a UNESCO Biosphere Reserve since 2001. The landscape on and around the Waterberg plateau is wild and typically African. Vast savannahs with thorn trees and scrub bushes alternate with rugged steep mountain ridges, deep gorges and plateaus. Only a few asphalted roads wind their way through the region. This South African province is in the north of the country and borders onto Botswana, Zimbabwe and Mozambique.

The Krüger National Park is one of the most famous national parks in Limpopo. There are fierce storms in the rainy season that create numerous small rivers and ponds. The landscape is shaped in equal measure by the environmental conditions and

the savanna, a combination which attracts a large number of animals, providing them with a natural habitat and hunting grounds. The climate is subtropical, so it requires some acclimatization. But in the African winter, when the marathon takes place, the weather is generally mild.

Zigzagging between the zebras
The start and finish of the marathon is at Lakeside Lodge, one of the largest lodges in the region that provides the comfort of a luxury hotel in the African wilderness. At the same time these lodges still convey something of the pioneering spirit and romance of the African wilderness.

A good example is Ravineside Lodge, which the runners pass after about 1 mile (2.5 km) at an altitude of about 400 ft (120 m). The lodge consists of various buildings erected on stilts on the hillside. Guests are not allowed to leave their room on their own to go to the main building; they must be accompanied by a specially appointed gamekeeper to protect them on their short journey to and fro. The region is free of malaria so it is not essential to be vaccinated it before travelling there.

The marathon route continues towards the Entabeni monolith, an impressive rocky outcrop of eroded sandstone that is part of every tourists excursion to the region. The route then takes the runners across a plateau before descending again through the Yellow Wood Valley across a narrow road section within the reserve. It becomes apparent why there are so many different zones of vegetation in this reserve. The difference of altitude between the plateau and the savannah is over 2,600 ft (800 m); but in the case of the marathon route, this difference is 1,650 ft (500 m) since the route goes

first downhill, then again steeply uphill. In total, the uphill parts of the route amount to 3,300 ft (1,000 m).

The Yellow Wood Valley is narrow, wedged between steep rocky walls. The dusty, stony road is very tough on the runners but the cycads provide a moderate amount of shade. Anyone meeting a rhinoceros here is advised simply to continue running and make as little noise as possible. These creatures are said to be friendly although they can run at over 30 miles an hour (50 km/h) if they want to. A runner catching sight of a rhinoceros or zebra, a giraffe or a wild cat should be excited about this rare encounter and not be afraid. You should only be concerned if you do not see a ranger nearby. They are positioned at close intervals to ensure the safety of the runners.

"It says on the street sign: 'Caution, lions!'"

A Kenyan runner, when asked why so many elite runners are from Kenya.

INFORMATION

DATE June

PARTICIPANTS About 120 starters

CHARACTER OF THE ROUTE This route is rugged and takes the runners across nature trails. Flat stretches are the exception here and the elevation gain is demanding right up too the finish. The Big Five Marathon is a real experience, and it is seen as such by the participants.

ENTRY FEE $270 (£160)

THE REGION The event is organized by the Danish company Albatross Travel and most participants book a travel package. This would include a tour of the "Big Five" game reserve as well as entry in the marathon itself. The region is about three hours north of Johannesburg and it is just what one imagines a game reserve looks like.

TIP FOR RUNNERS It may seem obvious, but it has to be said: Don't go running just

anywhere! And never go running alone. In a game reserve such as this one in the Limpopo region, the message sent out by a runner could be completely misunderstood by the wild animals. They would see it as a threat and react accordingly.

CONTACT DETAILS

Registration is through a tour operator.

Rio de Janeiro Marathon

Beachcombers under the Sugarloaf Mountain

Carnival, Sugarloaf Mountain, Copacabana: Rio de Janeiro's name alone conjures up all kinds of pictures. Few places have such evocative power and the marathon does much to enhance it.

The fantastic city of Rio on the spectacular Atlantic coast attracts many amateur runners, and elite runners are happy to accept the invitation, even though conditions are not ideal for fast times.

The city of Rio is defined by its several contradictions. And perhaps, as is often the case, this is what makes it so irresistible, so delightful and so appealing. Rio de Janeiro is rich and poor at the same time. Some 30 percent of its estimated six million inhabitants live in poverty and the city's favelas or slums are known throughout the world. But cultural life is rich: nowhere is the festival of Carnival celebrated with such impressive displays and nowhere do people samba as they do in Copacabana. Few cities in the world boast such famous landmarks as Rio de Janeiro with its Sugar Loaf Mountain and the statue of Christ 125 ft (38 m) high on top of the Corcovado peak. These are among the city's must-see sights.

In the shadow of the Sugarloaf
The marathon takes place in July, the season when the weather is coolest since Rio is in the southern hemisphere. Nevertheless, it is still very warm with daytime temperatures that can climb up to 86°F (30°C) in

the shade. It can also rain but this does little to cool the body because of the heat. But with a little luck the day of the marathon will be clear with a light wind and a temperatures of about 68°F (20°C). Such conditions are pleasant for runners because long sections of the marathon route run along the coast where the Atlantic breezes are favorable for running.

The start of the marathon is at Recreio dos Bandeirantes, location of one of the city's famous beaches, several of which are included in the marathon route. Runners are taken to the start by bus. The route is a point-to-point one so runners do not return to the point of departure: the finish is in the Flamengo district in the centre of Rio. Most of the route follows the coast, so runners will see the various colorful activities taking place on the sandy beaches.

Life on the beach is an integral part of everyday life in Rio. It is where people meet, where they play football and volleyball, where they eat, surf, rest and play. The beach near where the marathon starts is especially known as popular as a surfing spot. People's enthusiasm for sport is enormous.

Many of the locals come and take part in one of the shorter races. Here the marathon is very family-friendly—and also geared to amateur runners because besides the half-marathon, there is a also a 3.72 mile (6 km) race. In addition, sporty spectators often join the marathon runners and accompany them excitedly in all kinds of ways—on a bike, on inline skates but sometimes on a moped or in a car—until this was stopped by the organizers. The encouragement and enthusiasm of the spectators depend very much on the weather. When it rains, everyone in Rio stays at home. On the other hand, if the beaches are crowded, there will also be many spectators along the route who cheer and encourage the runners.

From Ipanema to Copacabana

The beach at Ipanema is followed by the even more famous Copacabana beach which is always crowded with bathers and sunbathers. At the end of the beach the route turns off towards the centre of the city and Botafogo Bay. Sugar Loaf Mountain is now within reach and large numbers of runners stop to take pictures of themselves in front this impressive backdrop. Then the runners reach the finish line which is on Flamengo Beach on the bay of Guanabara. There the crowds are partying and the runners soon forget their tired marathon legs as they react to the cheerful mood of the spectators.

"Finishing a marathon is more than a sporting success. It gives you the confidence that everything is possible."
John Hanc

INFORMATION

DATE July

PARTICIPANTS About 16,000 starters

CHARACTER OF THE ROUTE A mostly flat point-to-point race along the famous beaches of Rio. The white sandy beaches and luxuriant tropical vegetation are the distinctive features of this marathon, combined with cheerful spectators and samba music.

ENTRY FEE From $80 (£45)

THE CITY Rio de Janeiro is the second-largest city in Brazil and it radiates a real South American atmosphere. The main attractions are easily discovered on the your own but organized travel to the marathon often offers a more efficient timetable.

TIP FOR RUNNERS Runners in the future should plan their travel dates very carefully!

In 2016 the Olympic Games will take place in Rio.

CONTACT DETAILS

Maratona do Rio
Rua Felix Pacheco 150 Bldg C Apt. 102
Leblon 22450-080
Brazil
Tel.: +55/21/22 23 27 73
E-Mail: maratonadorio@maraton
adorio.com.br
Internet: www.maratonadorio.com.br/en/

Swissalpine Marathon

More than a race

The challenge of running a marathon is always compared to other demanding achievements. And often the parallel is made with mountain climbing. This comparison is spot-on in the case of the Swissalpine K42 Marathon since it combines both challenges: distance and altitude.

The combination of varied Alpine scenery and ideal running conditions is perfect for the participants (top and bottom). Runners crowding the Sunniberg Bridge in Klosters are an impressive sight (center).

This marathon combines distance and an elevation profile that frightens off the novice and commands respect from experienced runners: an impressive elevation gain of 6,037 ft (1,840 m) and an elevation drop of 5,512 ft (1,680 m). The marathon's route captivates the imagination of runners because of its demanding fitness requirements and its breathtaking scenery. But be careful: the Swissalpine K42 is undoubtedly one of the most challenging marathons. On some sections of the route the participants will be running on narrow, exposed paths in the high Alps. The route also includes stony mountain tracks and Alpine roads, crossed by melting ice streams and fields of snow.

Arriving by train

The start of the marathon is in the picturesque little village of Bergün, situated at an altitude of 4,478 ft (1,365 m) and reached by train. It is here that the ultramarathon runners of the K78, who started in Davos, join the route;

they are taking part in a demanding ultramarathon that is as legendary as it is unique. The runners then all progress together along the steep uphill and downhill route to the finish in Davos. The route goes above the tree line and along rock ledges through a landscape punctuated by steep, rocky outcrops and grassy paths with boulders. A rocky trail climbs up to the Keschhütte (mountain lodge) that is situated on a ridge at a height of 8,635 ft (2,632 m). Reached after 11.18 miles (18 km), the lodge lies as if it had been blown there in the wind. Most runners are reduced to a walking pace as they climb up the hill. At the top they will find a refreshment point offering welcome warm drinks. Here snow still lies even in July and the perceived temperature is often below 32°F (0°C) because of the wind chill factor, so every runner must carry a wind-resistant jacket.

After the mountain lodge, there are two route variations that have alternated in the past, depending on weather conditions. The slightly easier

one begins after a descent of 1,640 ft (500 m) down and a similar climb up again to the windy Scaletta Pass with part of its rocky trail covered by snow even in summer. The other variation is a more classic, more Alpine route leading to the highest point, the Sertig Pass at an altitude of 8,986 ft (2,739 m). It is reached after a steep, final climb 14.6 miles (23.5 km) long. The reward is a spectacular view of the magnificent Albula Alps.

Downhill at last

After the Sertig and Scaletta Passes, it is downhill all the way. In the next 2.5 miles (4 km) there is an elevation drop of 1,969 ft (600 m) and even experienced runners will feel their knees

tremble. The last 8.69 miles (14 km) downhill are less steep and bring the runners on paved roads to Davos where the marathon finishes in the stadium, tightly packed with spectators who welcome every runner like a winner.

The route of the K42 requires prodigious concentration and sure-footedness. Nor should the climatic conditions be underestimated. Runners who live at lower altitudes will notice their heart rate increases perceptibly even at an altitude of 4,600 ft (1,400 m). Because the air is thinner and most runners are not acclimatized to it, the body must transport the blood faster to ensure that there is sufficient oxygen in the blood, so the heartbeat increases. Also, the temperature drops

In the various track variations at Davos the highest point is the route leading to the Sertig Pass, 8,986 ft (2,739 m) above sea level. Many runners tackle these slopes.

81

The views on the course are spectacular (top). A narrow path runs along the Zügens gorge (center). It also passes through tunnels carved out of the rock (top right). At higher altitudes snowfields are common (bottom).

as the altitude increases. Temperature differences of 68°F (20°C) between the valleys and the high passes are not unusual on the marathon route.

The fascination of the Alps

Switzerland is renowned for its Alpine landscapes so it is natural that routes in running events such as the Swiss Alpine Marathon and the Jungfrau Marathon held in September should take advantage of this topography that is an attraction in itself.

For many runners the challenge of this mountain race is not the time taken but the running experience itself. This is not always predictable, even with the enormous logistical efforts deployed in Davos. In a race like the K42, the runners will pass through several climate zones and the runners have to take the external conditions as they find them. It has happened that some runners have been caught in such bad weather conditions on the Scaletta Pass that they had to take refuge in a sheepfold.

Additional races

The Swissalpine Marathon is world-famous and participants come from about 50 countries. So the atmosphere is very international and since 1986 there has an additional event, the K78 ultramarathon which is a prestige race attracting the international elite of mountain and trail runners. Birgit Lennartz, the former 62 miles (100 km) Road record holder and several times German marathon champion, has taken part in the Swiss Alpine Marathon ten times and won it every time, more than any other female runner. Nonetheless,

she admitted that when she first competed she did not know what lay ahead. "Otherwise perhaps I might not have taken part!"

In recent years over 4,000 runners have participated in the various races because ever more events have been added, some of them enabling less experienced runners to enjoy the experience. The new C42, the cultural marathon, follows a route with an elevation gain of 3,281 ft (1,000 m) that is just as exciting as that of the K42. "The cultural marathon goes through the most delightful scenery," the organizer explain. There are magnificent sights such as the Zügen Gorge and viaduct and the finish in Bergün, to mention but two. The route is a point-to-point race that starts in Davos and the full distance is only for experienced runners.

Marathon novices who are not sure that they would be able to complete the full course can nevertheless take part and cross the finishing line at Filisur. In this case they will be simply be classed by the organizers as having taken part in the K30 race, a race in its own right.

A perfect event for novices

This can also be a welcome alternative if—as often happens—it is particularly warm on the day of the race. In the C42 the first 6.21 miles (10 km) are on almost flat terrain, then after a slightly uphill stretch to 8.69 miles (14 km), the route is slightly downhill across nature trails until the distance of 18.64 miles (30 km) is reached. Here the runner must make a decision, whether to cross the finish line now or to continue for another 7.45 miles (12 km) for the full marathon distance with a small elevation gain.

Often the pleasure of running here is enough to decide to continue: the C42's combination of varied Alpine scenery and excellent running trails create perfect conditions enabling even a well-trained flat-terrain runner to tackle the marathon in spite of the altitude of 3,281 ft (1,000 m). The great advantage of the C42 is that there are no long downhill stretches. In mountain marathons it is these stretches that worry runners who are not used to them. They run more slowly but are less able to cope with the increased stress. The C42 is almost the perfect starter event for runners who would like to try a mountain marathon.

After the C42 comes the K21, a beautiful mountain half-marathon that rounds off the program. The scenic route of the K21 is a great attraction. Immediately after the start, the route crosses the slender Sunniberg Bridge 550 yards (550 m) long near Klosters, a fantastic experience.

"For me, a race is the same as a party"
Bill Rodgers

INFORMATION

DATE End of July

PARTICIPANTS In all, from 4,000 to 5,000 starters

CHARACTER OF THE ROUTE Besides the classic 42K-mountain marathon, there are also other race distances available, shorter or longer, for the novice or the pro. All these races take place in the magnificent alpine mountains and along specatcular routes, for instance across the Wiesner Viaduct, the Sunniberg Bridge at Klosters and the romantic Zügens canyon near Davos. The train journey to and from Davos is an experience in itself.

ENTRY FEE From $77 (£46)

TIP FOR RUNNERS Davos is one of the top vacation destinations in Switzerland so combining running with a vacation is an obvious thing to do. Inclusive trips are available combining marathon registration with a stay of a few days.

Davos is situated in the Grisons at an altitude of over 4,900 ft (1,500 m) and it is famous both as a health resort and ski resort. Runners are well advised to acclimatize themselves for a few days before the race. Many top runners come here for altitude training. For amateurs mountain walking is excellent training.

CONTACT DETAILS

Swissalpine
Postfach 536
7270 Davos Platz
Schweiz
Tel.: +41/81/401 14 90
Fax: +41/81/401 14 89
E-Mail: info@swissalpine.ch
Internet: www.swissalpine.ch

Running and enjoying the landscape often go hand in hand.

The fascination of marathons
Why 26.2 miles (42.195 km)? Three reasons

What is it that is so fascinating about a marathon? Clearly this book gives you 42 reasons, 42 places where the runners will enjoy a unique running experience. Visiting faraway places, traveling to foreign countries and discovering breathtaking landscapes is incredibly fascinating. Big cities close off large areas, organize music bands and entertainment programs. Streets, boulevards and eight-lane highways are closed to the traffic and thousands of spectators gather along the route to cheer on the marathon runners like heroes. That is the first reason, and in itself it is enough.

But there are two more reasons that may not be so obvious. Clearly it is not just the location that engourages runners to take part in a marathon. Another reason is the act of running itself. People love running, and because of their genetic make-up they are good at it. Nothing else could explain why thousands of marathons are organized worldwide every year—in the US alone there are 600 a year and over half a million people complete a marathon.

An old discipline back in fashion
Running is a booming sport but long-distance running is not a new invention. Quite the opposite. It appear to be one of the oldest

sports disciplines in which people compete against each other. Only the motivation has changed. The health-promoting aspect has only become important since about 1965. And the fact that running helps reduce psychological stress is a relatively new discovery, another recent encouragement to run.

"Stress" as a concept relating to people has only existed since 1936—both as an invention and as a recognition of the demands that modern society makes on people. Running was discovered as a treatment for problems caused by today's lifestyle, that is to say, as way of dealing with the conditions imposed by civilized societies.

Being good at running is one the defining features of the human's powerful brain. Of all living creatures, humans are among the best endurance athletes. Running is—or rather was in the pre-agricultural past—their recipe for success: their sustained hunting whereby preys could be pursued over a long time was an important factor in the evolution of the hominids.

This raises the question of the importance of human endurance from an evolutionary point of view. Is there perhaps a connection between erect walking and fast, endurance running on two legs, associated with the development of new skills and brain growth? In any event the evolutionary overall package has proved unbeatable: the combination of brain and endurance skills. To put it crudely: the ancestors of modern man could run well—but they also had the brain to use shortcuts in pursuit of therir prey.

Fuel for 18.64 miles (30 km)

In fact the shortcuts did not even have to be particularly short because man as a hunter had a radius of action of over 18.64 miles (30 km). From an evolutionary point of view this was apparently sufficient to exhaust the prey and kill it. People can travel such distances relatively easily. Humans have the necessary physiological requirements: the "fuel tank" of stored glycogen, that is, the quickly available source of energy, is exactly right for this distance. No animal can keep up with man for such a long time; it gets tired and so becomes an easy prey.

But here is the interesting part: the marathon is run over a longer distance than 18.64 miles (30 km), longer than the stored glycogen will last. A coincidence? Certainly not. Because that make it too easy. As top runner Bobby Magee (United States) said: "Anyone can run twenty miles. It's the next six that count." In other words, everyone can run 18.64 miles (30 km) and the toughness of the marathon starts at that point. If it was so easy, everyone could run the marathon.

The Olympic marathon winner Frank Shorter put it simply with a big sigh: "Why couldn't Pheidippides have died after 20 miles (32 km)?" Hard work and enormous efforts are part of marathon running. And talent does not come amiss. But for long-distance running, talent alone is not enough—it must encouraged and worked on. One is born a sprinter but one only becomes a long distance runner through training.

Impossible without training

What happens during training? Running has a wide range of effects on the whole body. Among the most important is the development of the cardiovascular system and the muscular system as well as the adjustment of the whole locomotor system: tendons and ligaments as well as bones and joints gradually adapt to the increased stress that occurs during running. In addition, the body weight also adapts: people who run lose weight. But there is another important aspect of long distance running: the nutrient supply to the body. This can be described from various points of view, physiological, technical, dietetic and theoretical.

Basically, the point is that the body has several kinds of energy supplies. These are complex processes that take place automatically during each activity. Whether the person is moving or resting, sleping, walking, driving a car or runing. There is also basal metabolism, the amount of energy that a person needs simply to

From 18.64 miles (30 km) it gets hard.

In a marathon, every runner is a star.

get through the day. Metabolism increases the more active one is. A builder needs uses more energy than someone sitting at a desk.

And a marathon runner burns about 10 kilocalories per kilogram of bodyweight per hour, which is much more than a builder—not to speak of an office worker. To give you an example: a runner weighing 165 lb (75 kg) uses 750 kilocalories per hour—which in the marathon means about 3,000 kilocalories. But then the energy supply comes into play: in normal everyday life the body gets a large part of its energy from its glycogen supplies. These are quickly available and are mostly stored in the muscles and blood. They are enough for just over 18.64 miles (30 km).

The reserves are endless but hard to reach

But the body has planned ahead, as it were preparing for bad times by putting away some reserves in case of need. A kilogram of fat corresponds to about 7,000 kilocalories of energy. Therefore that amount is available. The problem is that the body cannot reach these

supplies so easily. Figuratively speaking: glycogen supplies are quickly available, like chocolate in the refrigerator, but fat supplies have first be taken out of the freezer and defrosted.

In a marathon, even if you had a nourishing and healthy breakfast beforehand, the glycogen supplies will have been used up after about 18.64 miles (30 km). When this happens it is as if the fuel tap has been turned off. The solution is to start burning fat.

But to burn fat—and the under-trained runner will be particularly aware of this—the body needs more oxygen. And this oxygen is no longer available to the legs. This may not sound like much when described physiologically, just like switching over to the reserve tank, but it is a dramatic experience when running. Suddenly it feels like having "a rubber band between my legs." "The head is willing but the legs are not following." Or even more dramatically, "the man with the hammer has arrived." This is indeed what it feels like. Many marathon runners will be able to tell you this. And at the same time that the legs refuse to move, the mind also starts to play up. This results in an exceptional physiological situation that many people running a marathon have never before experienced. The temptation just to stand still is enormous, and the desire for quickly available nourishment is even greater. It is a transcendental experience. Many marathon runners report the drama of the situation, experiencing almost extrasensory moments, a runner's

"high." Many have what could be described as an epiphany—which sometimes even changes their life. "Marathon teaches you humility," as a famous writer once put it. Runners will not experience this when running a 6.21 mile (10 km) race, or even when running a half-marathon. It must be the marathon distance. And that completes the second part of the answer to explain why the marathon is so fascinating.

The distance, a myth

The third part is less physiological and psychological, therefore more mythological, perhaps even philosophical. The length of the marathon distance we run today is a historical coincidence. Or rather the combination of several coincidences.

The story of the origin of the marathon is based on a legend: the legend according to which a Greek messenger by the name of Pheidippides ran all the way from Marathon to Athens to announce the victory of Miltiades's army over the Persians in the Battle of Marathon. This is supposed to have happened in 490 BC. But it is a legend which—it must be admitted—we marathon runners like to believe and perpetuate, because it is a good story, even if it is made up. The battle did indeed take place near Marathon. The Greek historical writer Herodotus, born six years later, wrote about the 6,400 Persians killed in the battle and the messenger Pheidippides—but not about him running from Marathon to Athens. Five hundred years later this detail was expanded on by Plutarch while a century later the

Syrian writer and satirist Lucian picked the story and embellished it even further.

Where do the extra 213 yards (195 m) come from?

Running messages was a common form of communication. According to Herodotus, Pheidippides had already run from Marathon to Sparta, some 385 miles (240 km) in order to ask for military help. The next day he was back in marathon. So it does not seem likely that he would have collapsed after the comparatively measly 23.6 miles (38 km) from Marathon to Athens.

The marathon legend was revived again in 1896 by the first Olympic Games of modern times. Admittedly there had been other Olympic Games which had taken place earlier that century. But it was in 1896, at the Olympic Games in Athens, that the idea of including a long distance running race in the Games—in addition to the jumping, throwing, sprinting and middle distance running events—was first accepted. The Greek athletes took their training preparation very seriously. Of the 18 marathon runners who took part, 13 came from Greece. Along the route there was wine to be had and the villagers gathered along the road to Athens cheered the runners as they passed. Each runner was accompanied by his own escort on a bicycle.

The Greek Spiridon Louis only caught up with the lead runner, the Australian Edwin Flack, on the last and very hilly third part of the route. It is said that 70,000 spectators had crowded inside the Olympic stadium. Together with the King,

they witnessed the triumphant entry of their new national hero Spiridon Louis who won in 2:58 hours. It is true that at the time the route was only 24.23 miles (39 km) long. But the fascination with this type of race was born and in the years that followed marathons were organized in various countries including France, Germany and the United States. Usually the route was 24.85 or 26.09 miles (40 or 42 km) long.

Today's stipulated 26.2 miles (42.195 km) is the result of another historical curiosity: in the 1908 Olympic Games in London the length of the race was increased by 213 yards (195 m). The reason for this is that the start was in front of Windsor Castle and the finish was to be directly below the Royal Box in the stadium, which meant adding this distance to the length. Since then the distance of the marathon has been fixed at 26.2 miles (42.195 m). Imagine: a historical error. Simply because the finish had to be in front of the Royal Box, all marathon runners

now have to run 26.2 miles (42.195 km) instead of the original 26.09 miles (42 km).

It is always worthwhile

The marathon is loaded with symbolism—enjoying a challenge, getting the best out of oneself, pushing oneself to the limit, fulfilling a lifelong dream. But runners must also be aware: running a marathon is simply very, very arduous. And this should always be taken into consideration when planning to run a marathon, wherever it takes place. It takes up a lot of time, it requires a lot of training, it is physically very exhausting and it demands very good time management—as well as enormous determination and willpower to get through the sometimes painful physical strain, fatigue and exhaustion. This is an enormous challenge. But be sure that if you succeed in withstanding the pressure you will not be disappointed. It will be the experience of a lifetime and you will be the richer for it.

Crossing the finish line together: there is hardly anything that confirms a friendship more.

Finns are fans of the endurance disciplines, and of course the marathon falls into that category. The beautiful marathon route runs through the city center and the suburbs, both shaped by water.

Helsinki Marathon

Warmhearted when one perseveres

The Helsinki Marathon is well worth discovering by anyone interested in Nordic culture, beautiful landscapes and the Scandinavian way of life. The route consists of stretches along the water and through the town center.

Finland is not a country for eccentrics. The Finns are known as a straightforward, down-to-earth, unpretentious, inward-looking people. They do not exactly welcome strangers with open arms but after a short time they will open up. A particular trait is known by the Finnish word "sisu" that is found in the name of numerous clubs and associations. It describes characteristics such as endurance, will power, fighting spirit, toughness and patience, and it is therefore naturally associated with endurance running since it sums up all the mental and physical qualities that distinguish a long-distance runner. If someone asks what is typically Finnish, then "sisu," Sibelius and the Finnish sauna will all be mentioned in the same breath. It is a popular term that can be applied to an ice-breaker, an armored vehicle or strong throat lozenges. And the word "sisu" is also used when a Finnish long-distance cross-country skier, bringing up the rear with a broken ski stick, suddenly musters all his courage

shortly before the finish and crosses the finishing line as the winner. In short, in Helsinki the admiration for endurance is omnipresent. And this is why it is such fun to be involved in the Helsinki Marathon, the course of which is a pleasure in itself.

Finnish record holder

Finland's greatest Olympic hero was Paavo Nurmi, whose bronze statue o is not far from the start on the grounds of the Olympic Stadium. This man has been recognized as a long-distance running superstar since 1920; he was already habitually described in national and international newspapers as a "running wonder" and in Finland every child knows his story. He won five gold medals in the 1924 Olympic Games, two of them for his double victory in the 1,500 and 5,000-meter events. The amazing thing about this feat is that the two races took place within a single hour—and Nurmi set an Olympic record in both. In all he broke the world record twenty-four times. He carried the Olympic torch into the Olympic Stadium for the 1952 Olympic Games. Today this is where the marathon runners cross the finish line.

Immediately after the start of the marathon near Nurmi's statue, the route takes the runners in wide loop round the stadium before following the Helsinginkatur and the Mannerheimintie, two of the city's most famous main streets. After some 3.1 miles (5 km) the route winds its way to the waterfront with its marina.

Late summer light and a nautical atmosphere

The route then makes a wide loop, going through many little parks and across small islands and bridges, and also sometimes through an industrial zone or along the expressway. The route is bathed in a delightful late summer light that enhances the panoramic views of the sea along the seafront. Runners will see how the city of Helsinki has developed with new buildings on the little islands offshore, while the old brick warehouses have been converted into smart, elegant apartments. And here too there is a connection with the water. Going by the number of marinas along the marathon route, it seems that every Finn must have a boat moored in the city. During the Marathon in August the temperature can go as high as 82.4°F (28°C), but the constant sea breezes and dry air make this very bearable thanks to. And if it things are becoming too arduous: just think of the sisu spirit.

"We have no time, so slow!"

Paavo Nurmi

INFORMATION

DATE August

PARTICIPANTS About 2,000 starters

CHARACTER OF THE ROUTE The elevation profile does not contain any serious hill climbs. There are just a few small hills that are fairly steep, especially towards the end. In addition there are a few bridge ramps. Usually a light breeze blows in from the Baltic. Part of the marathon route follows the coast, going past beautiful parkland, then it passes by the parliament buildings and through some architecturally interesting parts of the inner city and the harbor.

ENTRY FEE From $77 (£46)

THE CITY In Helsinki one is very aware of the city's northern latitude, particularly in August when the sun only starts to set after 9 p.m. The city has a lively nightlife with pubs, clubs and bars bustling with people till late at night. For those who are interested, Helsinki is one of the major tango centers of Europe. Finns love this kind of music and there is a tango festival in February.

TIP FOR RUNNERS There are many running tracks in the city and along the coast that can be combined. A sauna and an ice bath can be enjoyed in winter.

CONTACT DETAILS

Finnish Athletics
Helsinki City Marathon
Radiokatu 20
00240 Helsinki / Finland
Tel.: +358/9/34 81 24 05
Fax: +358/9/34 81 23 67
E-Mail: marathon@sul.fi
Internet: www.helsinkicitymarathon.com

Autumn

Autumn is the most popular season for marathon events. There are two very good reasons for this: the climate is perfect for running in many places. It is no longer as hot as in summer and the air is fresh. And the previous months have been ideal for training for the marathon. This is why several of the most popular marathons take place in autumn, a prime example being the Berlin marathon.

Concentrated faces shortly after the start of the Jungfrau Marathon.

Don't take everything seriously! The Médoc Marathon is not about speed, but about socializing, enjoyment and fun. Many runners start in teams and they are not hard to recognize.

Marathon du Médoc

On a pleasure tour in running shoes

Here marathon runners can become acquainted with French culture in a very special way: the Marathon du Médoc takes place in one of the most famous wine regions in the world—and the wine is there for the runners to enjoy. And more.

When traveling to one of this most extraordinary of marathon events, you are also traveling to a region that is celebrated all over the world for its winegrowing estates and vintage wines. The district in which the marathon takes place in the part of France that contains famous appellations such as Haut-Médoc, Médoc, Listrac, Margaux and Pauillac.

The marathon starts in the little town of Pauillac, situated about 31 miles (50 km) north-west of Bordeaux. The region as a whole is bordered by the Gironde, a river that runs in a north-westerly direction before flowing into the Atlantic. The soil on the left bank of the Gironde is ideal for winegrowing. The excellent climatic conditions produce full-bodied, complex red wines, many of which are classified growths that fetch top prices on the international wine markets. Some of them will have matured for 20 years or more in oak barrels before being bottled, waiting for experienced connoisseurs to taste them and sing their praises.

A large proportion of these vintage wines is exported, notably to the United States and, more recently, China.

It was in this beautiful corner of France in 1984 that a group of enthusiastic wine-loving marathon runners had the idea of organizing a marathon. It is not clear whether they thought of this while running or while enjoying a glass of wine, but they immediately found a fine name for the event: the Marathon du Médoc. Proud of their region, they wanted to show all the participants the beauty of the countryside, so they devised a route that was a perfect combination of vineyard and landscape.

Winetasting included

But this was not enough: when running on soil that produces the best wines in the world, the runners should also be allowed to sample its production. This is

All sorts of wild characters are on the move in teh Médoc Marathon. The custom is to go as you like. In this marathon, anyone who competes in ordinary running clothes is missing out.

how the idea of involving famous wine producers in planning the route was born, so that it reflects the importance of wine in French society. And there are many famous wine estates around Pauillac such as Château Latour, Château Mouton Rothschild and Château Lafite, to name but a few. The marathon organizer has included sixty châteaux along the marathon route.

But the great thing is that there are wine tastings along the route, since about two dozen châteaux act as supply points during the race. In the first 3.1 miles (5 km) alone there are two wine tasting available and in the next 1.6 miles (2 km) there are a couple more. This continues all the way along the route. But because runners cannot live off wine alone, least of all marathon runners, there are a number of other supply points, well stocked with delicious things to eat! This is in addition to the many supply points offering water and soft drinks.

Oysters and steak

At the Médoc Marathon, oysters are served on white tablecloths! At 23.61 miles (38 km) you should allow a little time for this. After all, oysters cannot be eaten while running like a slice of orange that is sucked, then thrown away. No, they must be relished. So runners in the Médoc Marathon should not expect to make the best times. Over the next 1,100 yards (1,000 m), the runners pass several bands playing to makes the time go faster—before

encountering the next supply point at 24.2 miles (39 km): here they can enjoy a freshly grilled rib steak. And those who want to complete the meal in the French style can stop at 25.47 miles (41 km) where cheeses are served. Bon appétit! And perhaps ice cream for dessert? No problem: stop at 26.2 miles (42 km). Ice cream will indeed be very welcome because in mid-September when the marathon takes place, the temperature can climb to 86°F (30°C). And because the route goes through vineyards and villages, mostly on unsurfaced or partly asphalted roads, there is very little shade.

For those who may want to drink something other than red wine and water, there is also Champagne.

Red wine for runners?

The French suffer less from heart problems than most other nations. Some doctors and wine lovers believe that this is because of the French consumption of red wine. According to this theory, the phytochemicals contained in fermented grape juice lower cholesterol levels and protect the heart. Red wine contains certain volatile aromatics known as polyphenols, of which the most important is resveratrol. This is a substance that is present in the skin and seeds of black grapes from which red wine is made. A research group in Germany came to the conclusion that moderate consumption of red wine stimulates the production of adiponectin, a hormone that is thought to protect the heart. But this effect does not only occur with red wine, it is also found with moderate consumption of beer or an ethanol (alcohol) solution corresponding to a blood alcohol content of 0.03 percent for men and 0.02 percent for women. It is also often said that no less a figure than Spiridon Louis, the winner of the Olympic Marathon in the first modern Olympic Games in 1896 in Athens also stopped for a glass of wine on the way.

Be that as it may, perhaps the French also lead a healthier lifestyle, or there may be some other explanation for the fact they have fewer heart problems. Most people who drink a glass of red wine from time to time will be fine.

But this is not a license for excessive consumption of red wine or any other alcohol. Running and "boozing" do not go together. In the end it is like everything else in life—too much is too much.

"I've changed my addictive behavior. Before it was rampant gluttony and drunkenness, now it is running and body awareness. "

Joschka Fischer

INFORMATION

DATE Mid-September

PARTICIPANTS About 8,500 starters

CHARACTER OF THE ROUTE The Médoc Marathon is unique. On the evening before the marathon there is a banquet for 1,450 guests in one of the châteaux. Admittedly running is not entirely secondary, but here it is not considered so much as a sport but more as a way to move from one refreshment point to the next. The time limit of six and a half hours is generous. Every year there is a dressing-up theme such as carnival, historic, circus or science fiction characters and this is followed by 90 percent of the runners. In France a medical certificate is needed to take part.

ENTRY FEE $112 (£65)

THE REGION The Médoc region round Bordeaux and Pauillac is famous for winegrowing and as a vacation destination, particularly for the French.

For this reason it can be very crowded in July and August. The best time to visit is late summer and autumn when the weather is good and the grapes are bieng harvested.

TIP FOR RUNNERS Tour operators offer complete packages, including the journey, the marathon, excursion programmes and sightseeing tours. These are really worthwhile.

CONTACT DETAILS
Médoc Marathon Office
5, Rue Etienne Dieuzède
33250 Pauillac
France
Tel.: +33/556/59 17 20
E-Mail: marathon@agencetuttiquanti.com
Internet: www.marathondumedoc.com

Jungfrau Marathon
With bagpipes to the final climb

Switzerland loves its mountains and it looks after them. The Jungfrau is a fine example. But to run in the Jungfrau Marathon it is essential to be well prepared. A height of 6,003 ft (1,829 m) must be climbed.

The Bernese Oberland in Switzerland is breathtakingly beautiful and rightly famous. There are enchanting landscapes and rugged Alpine mountains, babbling brooks and rich green pastures with grazing cows, snow-covered mountain peaks and steep rock faces with the occasional red train travelling in the distance. Switzerland seems to have everything. This picture-postcard landscape is a reality and to a great extent it explains the attraction of the Jungfrau Marathon. The event has an enormous advantage: the Jungfrau region round Interlaken and the Bernese Oberland are popular holiday destinations, famous worldwide, attracting Americans, Europeans, Japanese and Chinese.

The tourist tradition goes back to the beginning of the 19th century and people who could afford it were coming to Switzerland even before that. Such a one was Johann Wolfgang von Goethe. On his second visit to Switzerland in 1779 he visited the village of Lauterbrunnen—today part of the marathon route—and was fascinated by the Staubbach Falls. It is said that this waterfall 974 ft (297 m) high inspired his poem "Song of the Spirits over the Waters":

"The soul of man resembleth
   water:
From heaven it cometh,
To heaven it soareth.
And then again
To Eerth descendeth,
Changing ever."

The cradle of tourism
Traveling to the Bernese Oberland and the ensuing tourist development were clearly accelerated by the construction of the Bernese Oberland Railway (1890) and the Jungfrau Railway (1912). Today many tourists still travel on the little red rack-assisted railway train through the Alpine landscape, enjoying views they would have otherwise never have been able to experience. Not everyone can be a marathon runner! The runners climb over 5,900 ft (1,800 m) but afterwards they can descend to the valley again using the Jungfrau Railway.

The first miles after the start in Interlaken (above) are level. Only in the second half of the course does it become really steep (bottom). Spectators can use the red Jungfrau Railway up to Kleine Scheidegg (center).

In planning the marathon route, Heinz Schild, the Swiss elite middle and long-distance runner, and his comrade-in-arms demonstrated that they had a flair both for running and for geography. The marathon starts in Interlaken at an altitude of 1,854 ft (565 m). The finish is on the Kleine Scheidegg, with an elevation of 6,873 ft (2,095 m). From here the runners have a breathtaking view of the world-famous Jungfrau mountain range 13,000 ft (4,000 m) high: the Eiger, the Mönch and the Jungfrau. Between the start and finish the runners will climb 6,000 ft (1,829

m) and there is also an elevation drop of 1,000 ft (305 ft). So runners who take part in this marathon must first study the elevation profile thoroughly; otherwise they will have the shock of their life—and will definitely never make to the finish.

But these facts convey only half the fascination of the route. The marathon has at least two sides to it.

Luxury from the start
The race begins in front of the Victoria Jungfrau Grand Hotel. Its luxurious pleasures include enjoying a drink of tea or coffee on the terrace

The air is thin at the top of the mountain, but the spectators encourage the runners tirelessly, whether with alpenhorns against the backdrop of the Eiger glacier (above), or with bagpipes on the moraine (below).

97

A procession of runners climb the steep moraine of the Eiger glacier (top). Someone has already found a good place to relax and enjoy the atmosphere.

on a mild, sunny September day or in the winter garden—after a successful run! Runners pass the hotel once more after the starting signal. The first short tour through Interlaken is as flat as the first 6.21 miles (10 km) to Wilderswil via Bönigen. Incredibly beautiful, especially in fine weather, the route winds its way along the Brienzersee lake and lush green pastures. Only then does the route start to climb but it does so quite gently. This is the real start of the marathon—the first 6.21 miles (10 km) could be described a warm-up run. The top runners are a bit scathing about this first part of the race, which takes them about 34 minutes at the most: for them it is quite a leisurely pace.

But then all hell breaks loose. Wilderwil is at an altitude of 1,926 ft (587 m), Zweilütschinen at 9.32 miles (15 km) is 1,139 ft (652 m) high and by Lauterbrunnen the height has already reached 2,697 ft (822 m). The next 3.1 miles (5 km) after Lauterbrunnen, which lead back to the village in loop in the course of which the Staubbach Falls come into sight, are completely flat. The runners have now reached 15.53 miles (25 km). At this stage it is important to keep calm and to avoid being distracted by the occasional base jumper leaping from the almost vertical rock faces. By now the runners can look forward to the encouragement of cheering spectators in Lauterbrunnen who reinforce their acoustic support by ringing cow bells.

Then the mountain looms in front of the runners. Shortly before 16.15 miles (26 km) are reached, the route bends gently and then suddenly the track begins to climb steeply. Here the uphill gradient reaches 18 percent: it is like running up a wall. After the relatively easy first half, this is where the battle starts for many runners—the battle against the mountain and themselves. A mental adjustment must be made here: running also means tackling steep climbs. There is no benefit in running fast because the effort required is out of all proportion. Because it is so steep, the route makes 26 zigzag curves as it leads to Wengen, although it is only 2.48 miles (4 km) away. This village is at 18.64 miles (30 km), by which point some 2,625 ft (800 m) have been climbed. Once again, it is an opportunity to enjoy journalist and former top marathon runner. The route is mostly flat, the climbs are extremely moderate and the elevation difference between the highest and lowest points is only 200 ft (60 m).

A meandering route with sightseeing

As with many with many city marathons, the numerous beautiful moments will remain engraved in the runners' memory long after the event is over. The route covers an exciting urban townscape with ever-changing views, overlooking the sea. The first half of the marathon passes through the eastern suburbs of the city and the popular Centennial Park in which the participants will cover 5 miles (8 km). It is in the

park that t
marathon
winds its w
hilly terrain
the city. Th
and Hickso
in the route
There are se
so runners v
others who
them; occas
rather crowc
The final stre
landmark, th
the finish. Th
food, drink a
place to celeb
with your frie

The whole
broadcast live
first time in 20

the amazing beauty of the Jungfrau region in summer.

Wengen is a picturesque village overlooking the Lauterbrunnen Valley. In summer this small village is comparatively empty but in winter it is full of tourists skiing.

Bagpipes

After a loop through Wengen, the route climbs steeply again, going past Allmend and Wengeneralp. It is not surprising that the uphill climb here is so steep because this is where the famous Lauberhorn downhill ski races take place. The runners will already be aware of the altitude because with every foot they climb, the air gets thinner and the pace slower. The route follows the terminal moraine of the Eiger glacier.

The glacier itself has retreated far back but the mighty ice mass is still impressive in the distance.

The climb across the moraine is tough. Most runners slow down here and hardly anyone overtakes. As if taking part in a procession, the runners walk painfully uphill along the moraine ridge. The atmosphere is completely different from that in other marathons, not least because the runners are carried along by the unexpected sound of bagpipes: at the highest point at the end of the moraine, at an altitude of 7,218 ft (2,200 m), a Scot is playing his bagpipes, encouraging the runners with their impressive, far-traveling sound.

And so they cover the last yards downhill to the finish line.

"Perseverance is the hardest discipline."

Buddha

INFORMATION

DATE September
PARTICIPANTS About 3,000 starters

CHARACTER OF THE
slightly up-and-down
impression of the city,
of many races in the S
Running for charity is
marathon starts at 7.2

ENTRY FEE From $135

THE CITY Although Si
is usually the first stop
Australia. The city is a
nationalities and the va
different from each oth
restaurants that enhanc
their varied cuisine. The
as Newtownm, where K
"Eat street" because of i

INFORMATION

DATE September
PARTICIPANTS About 6,500 starters

CHARACTER OF THE ROUTE To enjoy and complete this run, you must prepare yourself scientifically. The best time is held by the multiple world champion mountain runner Jonathan Wyatt (2:53 hours). Well-trained runners usually add about 40 minutes to their best time; less well-trained runnners should add about 2 hours. The route is almost all uphill without the downhill stretches that are so hard on joints and muscles. It is organized with typical Swiss efficiency: even the showers at the finish, at a height of 6,600 ft (2,000 m), are hot.

ENTRY FEE About $160 (£95)

THE REGION The first tourists first came to the Bernese Oberland in the 18th century. Today tourists come from all over the world. For

mountain runners the region is a real paradise in summer. Many valleys end here and the transverse valleys of the Bernese Oberland separate it from the high Alps.

TIP FOR RUNNERS Those who would like to experience the picture-book sights of Switzerland should repeat the second half of the marathon as a day's outing, then return to the valley on the Jungfrau Railway.

CONTACT DETAILS
Verein Jungfrau-Marathon
Strandbadstraße 44
3800 Interlaken / Switzerland
Tel. +41/33/827 62 90
E-Mail: info@jungfrau-marathon.ch
Internet: jungfrau-marathon.ch

Sydne

A running

Australia is a p

Few countries

House—which

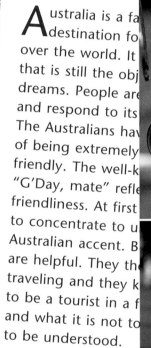

A ustralia is a fa
destination fo
over the world. It
that is still the obj
dreams. People are
and respond to its
The Australians hav
of being extremely
friendly. The well-k
"G'Day, mate" refle
friendliness. At first
to concentrate to u
Australian accent. B
are helpful. They th
traveling and they k
to be a tourist in a f
and what it is not to
to be understood.

Olympic tracks
For runners, the Sydr
the perfect opportuni
Australia. With its 3,0
has been integrated in
Running Festival that
35,000 runners in all a
three other popular ra
marathon, the 5.59 m
Bridge Run and the 2.
km) Family Run. All the

Running moments that will be remembered for ever: the sections passing the Sydney Opera House, crossing the Sydney Harbour Bridge and going under it.

In Berlin, the runners are cheered everywhere, particularly in Potsdamer Platz (top) and on the final stretch to the finish line after passing through the Brandenburg Gate (opposite page).

Berlin Marathon

Marathon in the runners' capital

The Berlin Marathon is one of the most popular marathons in the world. The long tour round the multifaceted city on the River Spree has many places of interest and historic sites. In addition, the route is fast, the organization is excellent and the atmosphere is perfect.

As the Governing Mayor Klaus Wowereit said a decade ago to sum up the city, "Berlin is poor, but sexy." He meant the city in general, which in spite of its economically precarious situation still conveyed a positive sense of life. It still does so today, and now it is prospering as well. It owes its special character to its lively cultural scene and the colorful mix of nationalities that give it an irresistible charm. All of this is reflected in the marathon.

Berlin was one of the first big-city marathons in the world and also a pioneer in the development of international marathons. Its history reflects the history of Germany. The first marathon took place in 1974; it was not in the city center but in the Grunewald forest, Berlin's green lung to south-west of the city. It was a charming runners' paradise close to the city—but in 1974 there were hardly any spectators. Running was still not a mass sport, far from it. People looked down on amateur

runners, looking askance at them or even mocking them. Sport as a health-promoting activity was not unknown but it was not popular.

A difficult start
In the early 1970s the German Amateur Athletic Association tried to mobilize the population with the Trimm-Trab "Keep Fit" Movement. Marathon runners were still considered weird creatures and a mere 286 runners took part in the first Berlin Marathon in Grunewald, most of them wearing cotton T-shirts and ordinary tennis shoes. Nevertheless this was a small miracle. With its wall separating West Berlin from East Berlin, the city was then the symbol of the divided Germany. The Western part was divided into three sectors with a strong military presence of American, British and French forces. The master-baker Horst Milde, an enthusiastic runner and the first chairman of the Charlottenburg Sport Club, used the small back room in his

Relaxing in the evening sun in front of the Reichstag (above). This is where the proud runners gather after the finish. After going through the Brandenburg Gate the finish line is just a few meters away (bottom).

bakery in Tempelhofer Damm to build up a small but efficient organization team. After skilful tactical maneuvering between politicians and the militaries in the various sectors, Milde managed to move the marathon route to the city in 1981. "At the time we were still considered crazy and the people did not understand what we were doing!" Horst Milde recalled. Nevertheless the marathon continued to grow while pushing for the development of city marathons all over Europe.

The route was moved ever closer into the center so that it could join up the tourist highlights. No other German city has so many imposing buildings, steeped in history, as Berlin, and the organizers know how to incorporate their city's places of interest in the marathon route. A good example is the Victory Column on the Strasse des 17. Juni which is passed soon after the marathon starts. Other conspicuous landmarks on the route are the Reichstag, the Europa Center, the Kurfürstendamm and the Kaiser Wilhelm Memorial Church.

An attractive route

The 1990 marathon was a real landmark in the history of marathon from both running and historical points of view. Three days before the official celebrations for reunification, the runners were able to run through the Brandenburg Gate shortly after the start.

And in the meantime the marathon has also become a prestigious event. The organization is excellent. For instance, there are few marathons of this size with such comprehensive

medical assistance. And last but not least the Berlin marathon is also famous for its enthusiastic spectators. The numerous bands hired by the organizers contribute to the festive atmosphere and the route now incorporates virtually every tourist highlight in the city.

The start is in the Strasse des 17. Juni. The runners can see the Brandenburg Gate if they look behind them! Shortly after the start the route takes the runners round the Victory Column. After the initial loop, the route continues into the Eastern part, going past the city's largest theater, the Friedrichstadt Palast. It passes through old, historical parts of the city but also past the Alexanderplatz and estates of prefabricated houses. The route also crosses the cult district of Kreuzberg and Neukölln in West-Berlin. And when things begin to get really tough for the runners and the "wall" is threatening, suddenly there is a large throng of spectators gathered on the Platz am Wilden Eber to spur on the runners.

A world record route

Several marathon world records have been broken on the almost flat route through Berlin. Many ambitious amateur runners appreciate the excellent running conditions: the temperature is mild, usually below 68°F (20°C), the air is dry and there is almost no wind. Top runners such as the Ethiopian Haile Gebreselassie and the Kenyans Tegla Loroupe, Patrick Makau and Wilson Kipsang (who set the world record in 2:03:23 hours) have all been hailed as heroes here. In 2008 Irina

Mikitenko improved her German record time in Berlin, completing the marathon in 2:19:19 hours.

By now the Berlin marathon had become very famous worldwide. In 2001 Naoko Takahashi was the first woman to complete the marathon in under 2:20 hours (2:19:46 hours) and since then the Berlin marathon has been broadcast live in Japan by Japanese television. Of the 40,000 participants, half come from abroad and over 130 countries are represented among the participants. And as running expert and sports event organizer Wilfried Raatz comments: the "organization is excellent."

There is a crowded. bustling atmosphere at the Marathon Fair in the buildings of the disused Tempelhof airport. With all its fringe events—from children's races to medical lectures—the Fair is an attraction in its own right. In the days leading up to the marathon, the pre-race nerves of the runners can be felt all over the city. Many runners are accompanied by their personal fans. About $100 million is spent in connection with the marathon.

Berlin was a pioneer in organizing of big city marathons and its role today as a marathon metropolis is confirmed by the fact that it is one of the six World Marathon Majors. The bib numbers for the 2013 Berlin marathon were sold out in just over three hours. For the future marathon 40,000 race numbers were available but twice as many runners applied. So who would take part was decided by the luck of the draw.

"I get the best ideas running and in the bath."
Florian Langenscheidt

INFORMATION

DATE Last weekend of Spetember

PARTICIPANTS About 40,000 starters

CHARACTER OF THE ROUTE A flat city circuit with many interesting sights through the center and its surroundings. Half the runners take more than 4 hours to finish the race.

ENTRY FEE From $84 (£50)

THE CITY Berlin has a cosmopolitan atmosphere with four universities, a vibrant art and music scene and the the metropolitan broadmindedness that makes it a perfect breeding ground for individualists. This is clearly reflected in trendy districts such as Prenzlauer Berg, Friedrichshain or Kreuzberg. Berlin has become a popular travel destination.

TIP FOR RUNNERS Hardly any other capital is so well displayed to runners passing through it. Highlights include the Berlin Victory Column (well worth climbing for the view from the top), the Brandenburg Gate, the Reichstag on the banks of the River Spree, the government district with the strikingly modern Chancellery built in 2001 and the Charlottenburg Palace in its delightful park. Berlin and its surroundings are perfect for running.

CONTACT DETAILS

SCC Events
Olympiapark Berlin
Hanns-Braun-Straße/Adlerplatz
14053 Berlin / Germany
Tel.: +49/30/30 12 88 10
Fax: +49/30/30 12 88 40
E-Mail: info@berlin-marathon.com
Internet: www.berlin-marathon.com

Toronto offers a flat and fast marathon course. A true high flyer has proved this: Ed Whitlock (below) ran the course in 3:15 hour as an 80-year-old, creating a class record for his age.

Toronto Waterfront Marathon

Flat, fast and festive

This marathon does justice to its proud designation of the Waterfront Marathon. Much of the route remains within sight of Lake Ontario. The lake has shaped the city with its cosmopolitan mix of inhabitants.

Toronto's skyline is eye-catching and impressively beautiful and to take advantage of this the marathon organizers have placed special emphasis on the lakeshore area. The running event started over 20 years ago and the marathon distance has been incorporated in the program since 2000. Before that there were only the half-marathon and the 5K race. At first interest in the marathon was rather limited.

But then word got around that the route in the Toronto marathon was fast and flat as well as picturesque. In 2003 the event attracted international attention in the press: the Canadian Ed Whitlock ran the Toronto Marathon in under 3 hours. This might seem unremarkable, except that Ed with his snow-white hair flying in the wind was over 72 years old at the time.

Remarkable records

He certainly set a world record in the M70 age group. In 2005 he improved his performance, completing the marathon in 2:54:48 hours, again in Toronto. As well as being a tribute to his endurance, this says a lot for the quality of the route and the climate in the city. "But of course I have time to train," he said succinctly at an event organized in his honor in New York. The magazine *Runner's World* voted him "Hero of Running 2005," a title of which he is very proud. Born in London in 1931, he has always been an enthusiastic long distance runner. As he said, "In England running used to be a much more important sport than it is today." He continues to set numerous records in his age group. In 2011 he completed the Waterfront Marathon in 3:15:54 hours—as an 80-year old.

But Whitlock is not the only senior citizen who has come to fame on the shores of Lake Ontario. The Indian Fauja Singh attracted even more international attention. In 2005 he ran his third marathon and improved his time to 5:40:04 hours. He was over 90 and the first such person to break the 6-hour barrier in the marathon. After the race, he said it was not particularly difficult. This was confirmed by his escort, who had to slow Singh down after he ran the first kilometer in 5:50 minutes instead of the planned pace of 8:30 minutes.

But you don't have to be 90 to enjoy this marathon. Toronto has proved its potential for best times and the route is undoubtedly a fast one. It is also a pleasant race to run since the weather in Toronto in early autumn is benign, similar to that of the French Riviera. It is on the same latitude as Cannes and one degree north of Boston.

A cosmopolitan city

Toronto is famous for its cultural richness and diversity, which is reflected in the marathon participants. The city has 2.8 million inhabitants, half of whom have been living in Canada for less than 20 years. There are many immigrants from South-East Asia, China and the Philippines; over 420,000 people in Toronto speak Chinese as their mother tongue. The city is known for its multicultural harmony and has claims to be the safest big city in North America. The marathon route goes through several districts of the city including Little Italy, the Caribbean quarter, Little Poland and Chinatown.

It is not only the spectators who create this exotic atmosphere but also the numerous music bands with their loud music. Here people of all ages enjoy themselves during the marathon.

"There are many reasons to run. The most important one remains: to find out who you really are."

George Sheehan

INFORMATION

DATE October

PARTICIPANTS About 6,000 starters

CHARACTER OF THE ROUTE A flat, attractive city circuit with two loops, starting in the center of the city. Mid-field runners cross the finishing line after about 4:15 hours. Both elite and amateur runners see it as a fast route.

ENTRY FEE From $84 (£50)

THE CITY Toronto is a very tourist-friendly city with a rich, wide-ranging cultural scene. This is even reflected in the marathon: there is a special brochure for spectators, the Spectator Guide, listing the best places to cheer and encourage the runners and also pointing out tourist attractions with transport tips. A dozen good places for watching are listed, so those who have accompanied the runners to support them will be able to enjoy the marathon to the full.

TIP FOR RUNNERS In spite of the size of the city, the runners will have many opportunities to discover it aas they run from the center of the city and then along the shore of Lake Ontario.

Trail-running in the center of the city is a popular sport here.

CONTACT DETAILS

Toronto Waterfront Marathon
264, The Esplanade
Toronto, Ontario M5A 4J6
Canada
Tel.: +1/416/944 27 65
E-Mail: info@torontowaterfront
marathon.com
Internet: www.torontowaterfront
marathon.com

Chicago is known for top times by the elite runners, but it offers an even greater stimulus for the amateur runner who will enjoy a magnificent impression of this typical American city.

Chicago Marathon

A very atmospheric city in the mid-west

The Chicago Marathon is one of the six World Marathon Majors and an IAAF Gold Label Race. The fast, flat route attracts many elite runners and many records have been broken here.

Chicago has a top-class reputation among elite runners. The event is extremely well organized, the route is flat and fast and the atmosphere along the entire route is unparalleled. Many national and international records have been achieved here, including world records such as that of Khalid Khannouchi (2:05:42 hours, 1999), who thus became the first runner to complete the marathon in under 2:06 hours. He had already caused a sensation in Chicago in 1997 when at the age of 20 he ran his first marathon—in the beginners' group—and set a distance record time of 2:07:10 hours. His bold performance immediately endeared him to many Chicagoans.

Several years earlier, in 1985 the British runner Steve Jones set a world's best performance with 2:08:05 hours, beating the Olympic winner Carlos Lopes and World Champion Robert de Castella. At the time 9,000 runners were already taking part in the marathon. Among the women the Kenyan Catherine Ndereba set a world record (2:18:47 hours) in 2001 which was broken the following year by the English runner Paula Radcliffe who finished a fantastic race in 2:17:18 hours.

Marathon experts like to compare the various international marathons and their elite runners. One such list is the average of the ten best performances in men's and women's marathons. At the top is the Berlin Marathon where the average for men in 2013 is 2:04:18 hours. As far as fastest times are concerned, Chicago is one of the top five fastest marathons. Many American runners choose the Chicago Marathon for setting their personal best performance.

Typically American and windy
For runners who are less interested in fastest times and elite performances, Chicago has an additional attraction. It is the archetype of the typical

American city with its giant skyscrapers, endless facades and tiny people moving at the bottom of its urban canyons. These urban canyons have an interesting side effect: they suck the wind into the streets. On Lake Michigan the weather is always perfect for sailing but the breezes of the lake are another reason for Chicago's nickname "the windy city."

Chicago is one of the biggest marathons in the world. The organizers accept a total of 45,000 applications, so the formalities before the start can take a long time and participants are advised to come early. The start and finish area is in Grant Park, between the Lake and the skyline of commercial towers and hotel skyscrapers. It is spacious and easily accessible, so many runners can walk to the start from their hotels.

After the start on Columbus Drive with its fantastic view of the city's skyline, the route first runs in a northerly direction. Because it is a circular course, it is easy for spectators to move around and watch the runners from different points. For the runners, one of the most enthralling aspects of the race are the ever-changing districts such as Chinatown, Little Italy, Greek

Chicago is one of the world's largest and most popular marathon events. The organizer accepts 45,000 applications.

Views of high-rise buildings and runners in deep urban canyons. Runners get to see the best of Chicago, hagh and low.

Town, Pilsen, South Commons and Old Town. Each mile is accompanied by a different musical band. In all the route goes through 29 different district of the city and past dozens of historic sites. The runners will see the best Chicago has to offer.

"Marathon Majors"

As a relative "upstart" in the Mid-West, Chicago has always been competing with the Big Apple on the East Coast for the title of leading American city. Early on New York became the financial capital with its many banks and the stock exchange. Chicago on the other hand was the capital of cattle breeders, stockyards and meatpacking, aptly described as the hog-butcher for the world.

But Chicago also wants to be in the lead so far as the marathon is concerned, so an entertaining rivalry has developed between the organizers of the two big city marathons. Then in 2006 there was a change of perspective and the five biggest marathons in the world joined forces: Boston, London, Berlin, Chicago and New York. This new alliance was called the "Marathon Majors" and in 2013 Tokyo joined as well. Besides cooperating in many ways, the Marathon Majors runs a competition with an annual jackpot of $500,000 (£360,000) each for the leading man and woman among marathon winners.

The year 2007 was notable for including the CEO Marathon Challenge. This was a subsisiary

competition between the CEOs of companies with a gross revenue of $5 million or more ($2.5 million for women).

In the first few miles of the race the runners will pass several interesting sights, with skyscrapers alternating with old brick buildings. During the first 3.1 miles (5 km) they cross the Chicago river three times—on a specially rolled-out carpet. After leaving the inner city center, the route continues along LaSalle Street and LaSalle Drive into Lincoln Park. The green spaces here are a paradise for runners with special tracks built for joggers—similar to those for cyclists. These go round the whole of the beautifully laid-out park as well as the zoo, one of the oldest in the United States.

The locals show a friendly admiration and respect for the runners that reflects the great popularity of the marathon. There are numerous aid stations with medical staff where teams of helpers hand out water, electrolyte drinks for rehydration and energy gels. They are professional and very encouraging, always having a cheerful word for the runners. The marathon is also very spectator-friendly with special transport laid on to take spectators to the various points of the race, so anyone who wants to accompany a runner can do so very easily in Chicago.

A party in every district

The reception is sensational in every part of the city with different groups competing with each other to give the runners the warmest welcome. Josef Ahmann, a marathon runner from Bamberg, sums it up very well: "I have never encountered such enthusiastic spectators at a marathon anywhere else in the world! Their cheers were so enthusiastic they gave you gooseflesh!"

But there is one peculiarity of the route that marathon runners should be aware of. Just as it is getting really tough, at about 19.88 miles (32 km), spectator support wanes as the route goes through a sparsely inhabited industrial zone. Then comes the final section of the route along the length of Michigan Avenue for 1.86 miles (3 km). Here there are plenty of spectators giving their encouragement.

The grand finale is the finish in Grant Park. All runners who finish within 6:30 hours will find their names in the newspaper, in the special Marathon section of the Chicago Sun-Times.

"If you want to win a race, run 100 meters. If you want to created a new life experience, run the marathon. "

Emil Zátopek

INFORMATION

DATE October

PARTICIPANTS About 45,000 starters

CHARACTER OF THE ROUTE This is one of the largest and most traditional marathons that first took place in 1976 and it is as popular as the New York and Boston marathons. Chicago's advantage is that the route is flat and fast, at least when it is not too windy or too hot. The temperature can be as high as 86°F (30°C), or even higher, as in 2007 when it reached 88°F (31°C). But usually running conditions are good, and the event is well-supported by an amazing public.

ENTRY FEE About $200 (£115)

THE CITY For a panoramic view of the city, take the elevator to the "Skydeck" visitor platform on the 103rd floor of the Sears Tower. Chicago looks fantastic seen from here. Visitors will find that the city is a fascinating blend of ethnic diversity and typically American lifestyle. Those taking part in one of the shorter races should plan carefully in advance and draw up a list of all the places of interest and cultural events they are interested in.

CONTACT DETAILS
Bank of America Chicago Marathon
135 S. LaSalle Street, Suite 2705
MC: IL4-135-27-05
Chicago, IL 60603
United States of America
Tel.: +1/312/904 98 00
Fax: +1/312/904 98 20
E-Mail: office@chicagomarathon.com
Internet: www.chicagomarathon.com

Munich Marathon

The Oktoberfest for runners

The Munich Marathon cannot compete with the biggest beer festival in the world. But the organizers have been clever enough to choose a date soon after the Oktoberfest, thus turning this marathon into one of the most popular destinations for marathon runners and fans.

In the second half the route runs through the old town, past the Town Hall (above). The first half of the course crosses the English Garden (center). The finish is in the Olympic Stadium (bottom).

A city of a million people that attracts millions of visitors every year cannot be sold as an insider's tip. But it is worth knowing that the Munich Marathon is not too big, a fact that makes it particularly attractive to runners and visitors alike. It may be overshadowed by the big-city marathons of Berlin, Frankfurt and Hamburg, but this counts in its favor.

Of course the city itself is already one of the main tourist magnets in Europe. Munich boasts magnificent buildings, from its ancient churches to its baroque buildings with beautiful ornate 18th and 19th century facades. The legacy of the Wittelsbach kings is everywhere.

But it also stands out with its buildings of the present day, such as Jakobsplatz with its strikingly modern Jewish Museum and synagogue and elsewhere the equally remarkable Allianz Arena with its exterior that can change color, the football stadium where FC Bayern Munich plays its home games. Its motto "Mia san Mia" ("We are who we

are") is a reflection of the Bavarian character.

The Munich marathon today it is becoming increasingly popular, an impressive feat in view of the strong national and international competition. It owes its growing popularity is to a unique concept that the organizers of the marathon have specially tailored for the city. They have moved away from the concept of attracting international elite runners and achieving top times. In recent years elite runners have not received appearance fees. So there is plenty of opportunity for "local heroes" to take part here.

The route is in fact perfectly suited for it: admittedly it is not absolutely flat and not super-fast, but it is ideal for the event. This is especially true of the finish. For amateur runners the finish alone is worth the registration fee: the last few yards are run in the 1972 Olympic stadium and the finish is directly in front of the main stand. Anyone winning the medal here will quite rightly feel a little like Frank Shorter, the 1972

Olympic Marathon winner who ran for the United States but was born in Munich.

Pretzels and beer

The runners will have become acquainted with the typical Munich atmosphere well before the start of the race, let alone before entering the Olympic stadium. A unique event takes place the day before the marathon: a "Costume Run" of 2.48 miles (4 km) followed by a Bavarian veal sausage breakfast with pretzels and wheat beer. It is a show not to be missed with the women in their dirndl skirts and men in lederhosen and traditional shirts,. On top of this, many visitors to the Oktoberfest seem to confuse the Beer Festival with the carnival and arrive dressed in the craziest costumes. Indeed, kimonos and kilts are equally popular here and many other national costumes are worn as well. Running shoes are the only thing people have in common

Organizer Gernot Weigl had the idea of organizing a costume run: "Since the marathon is about a week after the Oktoberfest, we simply extended it. This is why we have

Munich is where the German Marathon Championships are held. So many elite runners take part as well as amateurs who sometimes run in unusual outfits such as this.

Munich impressions. Whether it is the view of the Victory Gate (above), the costume run (center) or the finish in the Olympic Stadium (bottom), the Bavarian capital is full of variety.

beer and pretzels at the finish—just like in the Oktoberfest." And with a twinkle in his eyes he adds: "And just like after the marathon, there is wheat beer after the Costume Run," because the marathon runners are also given wheat beer after the finish. That fact is important for the organizers: "The runner must experience the typical traditions of Munich and Bavaria. Bavaria has a very strong identity and this is what we are also showing in the race!"

The concept is successful, as is reflected in the growing number of participants form other countries. One runner in three comes from outside Germany, most of them from Europe and some from America. There has even been a request to register from Japan.

The Oktoberfest

The Oktoberfest is the largest beer festival in the world, held in an enormous fairground. Running for sixteen days from late September to the middle of October, it is visited by about 6 million people.

It was held originally in October 1810 to celebrate the marriage of Crown Prince Ludwig of Bavaria to Princess Therese of Saxe-Hildburghausen. It is still held in the area known as Theresienwiese ("Theresa's meadow"), named for her. The beer is strong (about 6% alcohol) and it must be brewed within Munich. There are also many amusement rides and a wide variety of traditional food is available. The Oktoberfest is also widely celebrated

throughout the Unites States and in many other parts of the world.

Bavarian brass bands

The marathon route is in a scenic tour of the Bavarian capital taking in large number of landmarks and places of interest. The start is in the Olympic Park. From here the route goes to Schwabing where the first groups of spectators are waiting for the runners: partying starts here quite early in the morning and the atmosphere is terrific.

On the other hand, there are also several stretches without any spectators, such as the section through the English Garden where only dog owners and walkers seem to venture on the Sunday morning of the marathon. But a Bavarian brass band has taken up position at the Aumeister beer garden with its 3,000 seats, creating an authentic Bavarian atmosphere.

The mood reaches a high in the second half of the route when the old town is reached—which is also the more attractive, touristy part. Past the Gasteig cultural center on the Rosenheimer Strasse, the runners will see posters of prominent musicians and orchestras who have made guest appearances there. Immediately afterwards the runners approach the only perceptible slope in the entire marathon as it descends a few feet down to the Isar river. Here they cross the Museum Island, passing by the Deutsches Museum. A little later there is another change in atmosphere when they reach the Gärtnerplatz, one of Munich's hotspots. Numerous spectators have gathered here to cheer the runners who are also applauded by the many Sunday walkers on their way to coffee houses for breakfast.

Finish in the Olympic Stadium

The marathon runners will undoubtedly be impressed by the attractive city center, especially the Marienplatz where they are greeted by enthusiastically by spectators gathered along the route. Fascinating landmarks continue to punctuate the route: the national theatre, Odeonsplatz, the Maxvorstadt district with its art galleries and then the magnificent museum buildings of the neo-classical Königsplatz.

The runners will be familiar with the last 3.1 miles (5 km) since they are the same as the start of the race: they now return to the Olympic Stadium along the same road. In the last 1.24 miles (2 km) when the Olympia Park with the Olympiaberg, a hill with magnificent views, and Frei Otto's architecturally awesome Stadium come into sight, the runners are filled with a incredible feeling of exhilaration. They run through the tunnel before turning to the left for a final run round the stadium where the finish awaits them: goose pimples are unavoidable! Each runner crossing the finish line will feel like an Olympic winner.

"You train best where you are happiest."

Frank Shorter (United States), Olympic Marathon winner, Munich 1972

INFORMATION

DATE Mid-October

PARTICIPANTS 7,000 starters

CHARACTER OF THE ROUTE FA fat route with just a few climbs. The German Marathon Championships are held in Munich, a tribute to the quality of the course. The fringe events include other races (10 km, a half-marathon). The finish is always in the specatacular stadium, built for the 1972 Olympics.

ENTRY FEE From $80 (£48)

THE CITY As the lofals put it, Munich is a large village—even if the number of inhabitants belies this perception. This is particularly charming since Munich is in fact a commercial capital, a center of high technology and a Trade Fair city. And last but not least there are also the various festivals including the Oktoberfest, the Munich Beer Festival that is the largesin the world.

TIP FOR RUNNERS The southern part if the English Garden is a runner's paradise. The northern part is too, but here it is easy to get lost if you are not familiar wiht the area. The banks of the Isar River, both upstream and downstream, are ideal for longer runs. The flood plain on the left side of the river has some delightful trails that are usually uncrowded.

CONTACT DETAILS

Runabout München-Marathon
Boschetsrieder Straße 69
81379 München
Germany
Tel.: +49/89/17 09 55 70
E-Mail: info@muenchenmarathon.de
Internet: www.muenchenmarathon.de

There are few places that are not suitable for running. There is even a marathon at the North Pole.

Marathon tourism
The other way of discovering the world

Marathon runners are on the way: where will the journey take them? To the South Seas with its palm trees, to Osaka with its gingko trees or to Berlin's Unter den Linden? The range of international marathon events is large and varied. But first the runner must decide what the priorities are, whether it is marathon with a fast route or beautiful landscapes, with enthusiastic spectators or exotic surroundings.

The marathon provides the perfect opportunity for a city break or a trip to a far-off land on another continent. Every year several hundred thousand people travel all over the world to take part in marathons. Running travel agencies will organize journeys to the most distant corners of the earth—and of course to the big cities as well. Running events have become international meeting places. Indeed

several marathons have become known as fashionable hotspots for international marathon runners to meet up.

There is no absolute scale of the most popular marathons and this book has not followed a strict set of criteria in its choice of marathon events. If experts were asked to name the best events, they would probably agree on about one-third and have a reasonable discussion about the second third. As to the last third, the experts would certainly lock horns hopelessly. It comes down to personal opinion. Which is the most beautiful marathon? Where do people run best? Or run fastest? One might as well argue about where the most beautiful place in the world is to be found: in the Auvergne, in Africa or in the Caribbean? Or which is Europe's most beautiful château: Versailles, Sans-Souci or Linderhof? Or the most beautiful capital: New York, Rio or Paris? Where do you find the loveliest flowers or the most beautiful people?

Deciding which one to go for

Marathons can be rated mathematically—indeed such computations are commonly made to calculate certain aspects: best times, the most spectators, the numbers of participants and the costs of registration. But gut feeling is much more important and it is difficult to quantify since there are no criteria that can be measured. Many runners find the west coast of California beautiful, others prefer the South Seas, the South Pole or the Salzkammergut region of Austria.

The concept of the most beautiful marathon is therefore an individual matter and it also depends on the country. For instance, the largest foreign contingent in the New York Marathon is from France, in the Berlin Marathon it is from Denmark and in the Honolulu marathon from Japan.

Trust your instinct!

You cannot go wrong in your choice of destination if you rely on your instinct. Especially if you also take a few criteria into consideration. You must remember that your travel experience depends partly on your traveling companions who are also taking part in the marathon. It is the same with happy vacation memories: these are usually associated with people with whom one has shared special moments. With the right company anywhere can be beautiful.

It is important that marathon enthusiasts should be clear about their motives, hopes and expectations. The events described in this book should be seen as an encouragement to discover the world of marathons and to add a further dimension to this experience.

Most runners will agree that those who run see more of life, more of cities, landscapes and countries. Marathon runners have a lot of contact with people and they get an excellent insight into their own civilizations and countries. Runners from all over the world feel closer to each other and approach each other more easily. Of course, there are unfriendly people everywhere, but there are very few unfriendly runners. And wherever you travel as a runner, you feel accepted. Wherever you go will be made very welcome and cheered on

There are many different types of marathon runners. Many simply seek the fun of running.

enthusiastically by spectators at major running events. Marathon runners benefit from a sympathy bonus: anyone who runs cannot be bad.

This seems to be an internationally accepted concept among people anywhere. The author has felt this whether he was running in South America or New Zealand, Japan or Jamaica. And this is one of the most beautiful discoveries a runner makes: running is like a language, a body language that is understood everywhere. It is a kind of understanding and a form of communication. As runners you are sending out a message, you convey an impression of yourself; but at the same time you make contact with your surroundings.

For most runners it is things like this that really count. Technical details, such as target times, best times or the number of marathons run are personal statistics that are relevant to you. But even more important is what you have experienced and felt.

Choice and orientation

In order to help in choosing a marathon you can draw up a decision grid. For instance: Which of these four criteria is most important to you?

1. City or beautiful landscape: This is a simple choice with many marathons in either category— and some that combine the too.

2. The exotic factor: If you want to experience something special or run in unusual surroundings, you may choose the North Pole Marathon or the Great Wall Marathon in China.

3. Enthusiastic crowds: You will find the largest crowds of

Where do you want go for a marathon? There is hardly a popular tourist city in the world that does not have a marathon event.

118

Somewhere in the world there is always a run, still to be discovered.

spectators in traditional runs or big-city marathons. It is best of all if the event is both of these things, such as the New York, London or Chicago marathons. On the other hand, if you want to avoid large crowds and noise, it is better to choose smaller events in rural areas.

4. Fast routes: You want to run a personal best time? Then the criteria are simple: you need a flat route with few bends, a reliable climate and favorable running conditions. For instance, you could choose the flat marathon routes such as

Chicago or Berlin because that is where most of the marathon records are broken.

Preparing for the trip
Running a marathon is an extremely demanding sporting performance, so nothing should be left to chance. Plan your trip with the greatest care. Make lists of everything that is relevant. This includes every detail of the journey, your accommodation, the equipment you will take with you and also food supplies. What you eat is important in the lead-up to the marathon as well as on the day itself.

DECISION CRITERIA FOR MARATHON EVENTS
• Beautiful landscapes or city
• The exotic factor
• Enthusiastic crowds
• A fast track

You will not get all the carbohydrates you need from just a single dish of pasta. So pay attention to these details. When you have made all your plans and implemented them, you will enjoy the combination of traveling and marathon running to the full.

Maorca is a dleightful tourist destination, picturesque and friendly. The Marathon is run on the most beautiful squares and streets of the old town of Palma.

Palma de Majorca Marathon

The loveliest island marathon in the world

The popular destination of Majorca (or Mallorca as it is in Spanish) has its own marathon that combines all the typical aspects and impressions of the island: the old town of Palma, the cathedral of La Seu, the sophisticated marina, the sea and the endless sandy beaches.

Few holiday destinations attract such multi-faceted crowds of tourists as Majorca does. It is obvious that most people come here to relax, but there are many different ways in which this can be done. The endless sandy beaches in the south, the small pine-trimmed coves to the east and the bathing places surrounded by cliffs to the north and west make it a perfect place to enjoy the sea. There are over 180 sandy beaches awaiting visitors.

But at the airport, as well as numerous tour parties in flip-flops, there is now an increasing number of tourists in hiking outfits who have come to explore the interior of the island and the mountain landscapes. The highest summit, Puig Major, is 4,711 ft (1,436 m) high. The mountain range running from south-west to north-east known as the Serra de Tramuntana has many peaks that are more than 3,300 ft (1,000 m) high and it has been awarded the status of a World

Heritage site by UNESCO. As well as ramblers it also attracts trail runners. There are comparatively few traditional running tracks but the Majorcan mountains have large numbers of picturesque paths for people to enjoy the beautiful surroundings.

Ramblers and the runners are just a small proportion of the sports tourists who come to visit this beautiful island. There are cyclists, swimmers, triathletes, scuba divers and golfers. More than 8 million tourists visit the island every year and 80 percent of the islanders are involved in the tourist industry.

The marathon is part of an effort to widen the range of Parma's attractions beyond sun and sand, delightful as they are. The logic is that diversifying into sports events will attract more tourists spread over different parts of the year.

The marathon's main sponsor since its second year has been the German tour operator TUI. There are many promotional travel offers

centered on the marathon in which about 11,000 runners from over 60 countries take part. The marathon is both a physical experience and a holiday event, organized with a combination of Teutonic efficiency and Majorcan panache.

VIPs at the start

The marathon weekend involves several VIPs, such as the rock musician Peter Maffay firing the starting pistol in the Kids Run. Or Eckhart von Hirschhausen presenting a new play in Palma—and two days later donning his running shoes for the 10K race which takes place in parallel with the marathon. The self-proclaimed "King of Majorca," Jürgen Drews, will be there to ensure that the 10K run is well covered by the international press, and he will also be at the runner's party after the marathon in one of the famous clubs.

But runners who can forego all the VIP fuss will certainly get their money's worth. The route and the organization of the marathon perfectly reflect Palma's character,

Built on the site of a former mosque, the magnificent Cathedral of Saint Mary, known locally as "La Seu" is always in view of the runners (above). Palm trees provide some welcome shade along the route (below).

The marathon route seems to have been chosen for its beauty and the runners will have many happy memories of the setting to go home with. The weather is almost always fine as well.

as do the fringe events such as the Runners' Fair with the collection of bib numbers and the Pasta Party in the Parc de Mar, in the shadow of Palma's cathedral La Seu. Local craftsmen are invited to the Fair where they can present their typically Majorcan products, ranging from hand-made objects to herbs and spices.

The organizers describe it as the most beautiful island marathon in the world and the route certainly supports this claim since it has been largely planned around scenic criteria.

The start is near the cathedral in the Parc de Mar and from there the runners move in a westerly direction along the Bay of Palma. Then they pass the harbor and the exclusive Royal Yacht Club. The first 6.84 miles (11 km) are a turnaround route along the Avinguda Gabriel Roca.

After about 3.4 miles (5.5 km) the runners reach the first turnaround on the waterside promenade. There is not very much interest from spectators here: the Majorcans are going about their business, sitting at café terraces and looking on sympathetically, but perhaps too a little skeptically.

The most beautiful city in the Mediterranean

The loop back towards the start-finish area is beautiful with the majestic cathedral coming into sight at the 4.97 miles (8 km) mark. After a small detour round the harbor mole Camí

de S'Escollera—with a view of the elegant millionaires' yachts—the runners enter the magnificent Avenida d'Antoni Maura which takes them into Palma's old town.

Travel guides describe Palma as one of the most beautiful cities in the Mediterranean and visitors to Majorca should certainly not miss it. Here life is lived in cozy inner courtyards and magnificent palaces, surrounded by countless churches and bustling markets. There are numerous small bistros, fun restaurants and picturesque shopping streets—the marathon route runs right through it all, along streets such as the Passeig La Rambla after 7.45 miles (12 km). And beneath the old plane trees, the runners pass beautiful houses with balconies enclosed by elegant wrought iron railings. The flower market provides a colorful touch while elegant cafés inviting passers-by to stop, for instance at the "Bodega La Rambla," one of the best tapas bars.

The route winds it way through the old town, past central squares and boulevards and after some 10.56 miles (17 km) it runs behind La Seu, the beautiful cathedral that provides some welcome shade for the runners before they turn back into the narrow streets, crowded with passers-by.

Newcomers will probably be surprised by the zigzag lanes and alleyways, the stumbling on cobblestones, the old facades and narrow streets that necessitate sharp changes of direction. But here the true soul of Palma is to be found.

The sound of the sea as a musical accompaniment

This section through the old town has its pitfalls, especially when it is rains. October is the wettest month of the year, with an average of six days of rain. Sometimes it seems that it is always raining during the marathon… and then it is important to be careful because the cobblestones get very slippery.

After 11.80 miles (19 km) the route goes through the newer parts of Palma back towards the sea. In the second half of the marathon the route makes a wide loop along the coast in a south-easterly direction until the next turnaround at the 18.64 miles (30 km) mark. Then the runners are back on the coastal promenade, flanked on one side by endless sandy beaches and on the other by hotels and sangria bars—and , even more welcome to the runners, the cheering of holidaymakers accompanied by the sound of the sea. A perfect picture of Majorca: at the finish near the cathedral every runner will feel like the king of Majorca.

"We runners are a bit barmy, but we'redecent people."

John J. Kelley, Winner of the Boston Marathon

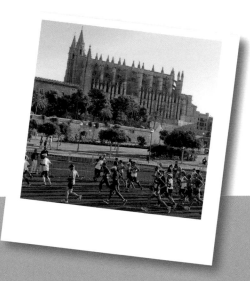

INFORMATION

DATE October

PARTICIPANTS About 1,800 starters

CHARACTER OF THE ROUTE The route could well be described as touristy but it does reveal the various faces of Palma, including its long, sandy beaches as well as the narrow streets in the old town. There are no long or steep climbs but the route in the old town is fairly twisty and the promenade along the sea can be quite windy. The atmosphere is light-hearted: for many runners it is a fun marathon rather than a serious competition..

MELDEGEBÜHR From $70 (£42)

DIE REGION The island of Majorca has succeeded in recent years to distance itself from its erstwhile image and now offers a wide range of holiday activities to a broad tourist spectrum. For runners there are many training - and running possibilities especially along the endless coastal promenades or alternatively on the attractive trails in the Tramuntana mountains.

TIP FOR RUNNERS Those on vacation should take advantage of the early morning hours to go and run: the light and the air are at their best then, it is still not too hot and as another bonus, the tourists will not have got up yet.

CONTACT DETAILS

TUI España Turismo S.A.
Avenida 16 de Julio, 73
07009 Palma de Majorca
Spain
Tel.: +49/1805/55 56 75
E-Mail: info@tui-marathon.com
Internet: www.tui-marathon.com

The start and finish of the marathon are in the venerable Olympic Stadium (above), which was built for the 1928 Olympic Games. Large parts of the route show a picture-postcard Holland with windmills and canals (center).

Amsterdam Marathon

Canals and green areas

The Amsterdam marathon takes advantage of the picturesque aspects of this city of canals. Marathon tourists are spoilt here with large numbers of enthusiastic spectators and the beauty of the course. The start and even more the finish in the stadium are quite unique.

The Amsterdam marathon has a long tradition. It has been taking place since the mid-1970s, always in October. As one of the great running events in the Netherlands, it is also well-known internationally.

Some 25,000 runners are involved in the running events in Amsterdam, the city of canals on the River Amstel. Over 10,000 of these are participants in the marathon with its picturesque route and crowds of enthusiastically cheering spectators.

The start is in the historic Olympic Stadium, built in 1928 and now a protected monument. Admittedly it is not in the center of the city but the very fast route swiftly takes the runners through the picturesque old town. Narrow lanes, tall, slender houses and of course the numerous canals complete the city's picture-postcard image which the runners will enjoy.

The route then takes the runners past the Rijksmuseum and the Vondelpark which as the largest municipal park is popular with runners throughout the year. They share this green space with many other enthusiasts: walkers and break-dancers as well as yoga and Kendo practitioners who can do their exercises here in the open: it is quite a sight! And as dusk sets in the park becomes a favored meeting point for lovers, as it has always been.

An impressive list of winners
The marathon route takes the runners for long stretches along the Amstel, and through green spaces. There is an atmosphere of modest grandeur which is reflected is in the elegant but unostentatious houses of prosperous merchants.

For a tourist runner the Amsterdam marathon is a rewarding destination and the other events includes a popular half-marathon and an 8K run. The meeting point and start for all the events is the Olympic Stadium, where in 1928 Boughèra Mohammed El Ouafi won the gold medal in the

Amsterdam Olympic Games marathon in 2:32:57 hours.

Today's marathon has been held regularly since 1975. In that year a Dane, Joerge Jensen, won the marathon in the impressive time of 2:16:51 hours. The following year it was won by the Belgian Karel Lismont who had already won a silver medal in the marathon in the 1972 Olympic Games in Munich. And in 1977 the marathon was won in 2:09:55 hours by the popular American Bill Rodgers, who had already won the Boston Marathon in 1975.

The list of winners continued to include prominent competitive sportsmen. The victory of the Dutch runner Gerard Nijboer in 1980 was spectacular and much celebrated since he had also improved the Dutch record by completing the race in 2:09:01 hours, at the same time setting a European record and running the second-fastest time ever run in a marathon. The Dutchman won four times in Amsterdam.

Always along the water

The route through Amsterdam conveys an atmosphere true to its picture-postcard reputation. The picturesque canals, the tiny, narrow squares and streets the ever-present water that is an integral part of the landscape: these are the aspects of the city that the runners experience along the route. As soon as the runners reach the periphery of the city, they are in equally beautiful rural surroundings. Here the route through the lowlands is lined with spectators and the atmosphere is euphoric.

"The most beautiful runs are not the fastest, but the one in which you realize how beautiful life is. "

Kara Goucher

INFORMATION

DATE October

PARTICIPANTS About 11,000 starters

CHARACTER OF THE ROUTE The route is mostly flat and goes through both the city itself and the suburbs. It is one of the fastest marathons in the world and attracts elite runners pursuing top times. There are numerous fringe events for those accompanying the runners.

ENTRY FEE From $84 (£50)

THE CITY The inner center of Amsterdam is like an amalgam of densely packed impressions. The city can explored in many ways, on foot, by boat or bicycle. A car is not recommended—it is the worst way of discovering the inner city center. The weather conditions in October when the marathon takes place are very pleasant and the crowds of tourists have greatly diminished by then, although there always seem to seem quite a lot of people milling around. Nevertheless, it is always possible to find a quiet corner.

TIP FOR RUNNERS Running round the Vondelpark in the centre of the city is a unique experience, one that rarely occurs in such a small area.

CONTACT DETAILS
Le Champion
Postfach 5029
1802 TA Alkmaar
Netherlands
Tel.: +31/72/532 48 49
Fax: +31/20/532 93 98
E-Mail: info@tcsamsterdammarathon.nl
Internet: www.tcsamsterdammarathon.nl

The start at the Trade Fair grounds. The fast route of the Frankfurt Marathon has made it a benchmark for the elite. Many runners strive to run a personal best here.

Frankfurt Marathon

A fast route with the "Hammering Man"

On the world marathon map a thick red pin is stuck in the city of Frankfurt. World-class performances and mass sports have been associated with the city since 1981 and in recent years this popularity has continued to grow. Frankfurt is one of the world's top marathon locations.

A financial center, the international airport, the stock exchange, the Deutsche Bank, the Fair—these bywords of commerce that today are automatically associated with Frankfurt describe only part of the quality and the character of the city. It is evident that Frankfurt is a transport hub with its airport that is one of the largest in the world, and the skyline of the city is defined by skyscrapers housing numerous financial companies and business HQs. But at the same time they hide the rich history of the city and its other qualities: for instance, the Frankfurt municipal woods combined with the paths along the banks of the river Main are very popular with runners. Thanks to their size they are perfect for long runs in preparation for the marathon, with no irritating zigzag stretches. Finding a training circuit of 12.42 miles (20 km) is no problem.

Pioneer on the marathon scene, but it was not the ideal training conditions nearby that in 1981 paved the way for the marathon to move to the center of the city. The running scene had not then developed enough to appear there spontaneously. The first jogging wave spread through Germany in the 1970s, attracting an increasing number of runners and leading to the organization of mass running events. But marathon running was still for experts, for ambitious sportsmen who often came from the track and field scene—and were often regarded as "oddballs" by the public. So the pioneering spirit in Frankfurt that triggered a change in attitude was all the more remarkable.

The organizers of the 1981 OSC Hoechst marathon, Wolfram Bleul and Hans Jürgensohn, were real visionaries. They were clever enough to enlist a powerful and influential sponsor, the Hoechst chemical and pharmaceutical company, which was able to contribute important infrastructure through its works grounds. In turn, Hoechst's image benefited from the marathon.

Developments in the chemical and plastics industry should not be underestimated in contributing to the

success of the running movement. At that time manufacturers of sports equipment were paving the way for the first joggers by developing running shoes with inner soles cushioned with synthetic material. In those years the main manufacturers of running shoes were Adidas, Puma and Brütting. Nike only arrived on the European market in 1978 and as far as the technology of running shoes was concerned it was still in its infancy. The first models were much sought-after, exclusive and considerably more expensive than the German products.

A promising premiere

There were numerous inexperienced amateur runners in the first Frankfurt marathon on May 17, 1981. They were simply taking part out of curiosity, standing next to seriously ambitious runners. Professional runners did not yet exist and the registration fee was very modest. The race started in the spacious grounds of the chemical company, then made its way towards the center of the city. "It really stank at the start in the factory grounds, I just wanted to be off," Eugen Föt remembered about the first marathon. Even so, he has continued to take part in his home

The Frankfurt Marathon attracts world-class elite runners. The city is often known as Germany's Manhattan because of the high-rise buildings in the center; but the route also goes past older buildings such as the Opera House (above).

Cheers and crowds at the finish. The last few meters of the marathon are completed on the red carpet in the Frankfurt Festhalle. In the 1980s (opposite page), the field was smaller, but comparatively much faster than today.

city's marathon, the last time being in 2013.

As it still does, the route went first towards the medieval Römer building, then across the Main and through the districts of Sachsenhausen, Niederrad and Schwanheim. What fascinated the runners in particular was the enthusiasm of the spectators. As a result of good public relations and posters, leaflets and radio announcements, there were a good 10,000 spectators gathered along the route. This had never happened before in Germany!

From a present-day perspective the performance level of the runners was also remarkable: 22 percent of the participants, that is, 568 runners, crossed the finishing line in under 3 hours, and in the following year the number doing so rose to 1,081. In comparison: in 2012, 890 runners completed the race in under 3 hours. But in 1981 only 2,588 runners took part, while in 1982 there were 4,677 participants and by 2013 the number had risen to 11,948.

So in the first two editions of the marathon the average performance level was even higher than it is today. Frankfurt is often used to make such comparisons because this race has always been a benchmark for the marathon elite.

Records

In the following years the level of performance continued to rise even further. In 1983 23.6 percent of the 5,117 runners completed the race in under 3 hours and in 1985 the number rose to 25.9 percent. Many major

records were broken in the early years of the Frankfurt marathon. In 1981 the Swede Kjell-Erik Ståhl won the race in 2:13:20 hours and 40 German runners finished the race in less than 2:30 hours.

By way of comparison: in 2012 two Germans completed the race in under 2:20 hours. Also noteworthy: the winner, the exceptional runner Kjell-Erik Ståhl, completed seventy marathons in under 2:20 hours in the course of his running career. The performance level in the Frankfurt marathon has always been of world class.

Wilson Kipsang's victory in 2011 was a real highpoint: he completed the race in 2:03:42 hours, only 4 seconds outside the world record and the second-fastest marathon of all time. The Kenyan was already showing his extraordinary potential which he confirmed two years later by breaking the marathon world record in Berlin.

What is so special in Frankfurt is that the elite runners do not just run ahead or aim to set records. They are such a large group that they turn the finish into a thrilling finale. In 2013 no fewer than 14 runners completed the race under 2:10 hours, a record result. In the women's event, 12 completed the race under 2:30 hours, another evidence of the high quality of the elite field.

A festive finish

As well as being an excellent marathon for setting best times, the route also includes several interesting features along the way. For instance, the start is dominated by the "Hammering Man," a statue of a worker 66 ft (30 meters) high holding a hammer in his hand. It is a wonderful emblem to mark the start of the marathon, particularly since "hitting the wall" is sometimes described as "meeting the man with a hammer." The route then takes the runners past the old Opera House and to Frankfurter Zeil, the city's main shopping street.

After some 16.15 miles (26 km) the runners reach the district of Hoechst, where the marathon had started in 1981. Then it turns back towards the city and after a loop it takes the runners into the Trade Fair Grounds. In 2003 the marathon organizer Jo Schindler moved the finish to the Festhalle there. It is a handsome building more than 100 years old: "We just wanted to create a unique finish. We can do this here because we can really provide a special atmosphere in the Festhalle, both for spectators and runners." Indeed, it is a fantastic feeling for the runners to run the last few yards on the red carpet inside the Festhalle where they are welcomed and cheered enthusiastically by 7,000 spectators.

> *"Happiness comes by itself, it is enough to sweat."*
>
> *Emil Zátopek, Czech running legend*

INFORMATION

DATE Oktober

PARTICIPANTS About 16,000 starters

CHARACTER OF THE ROUTE The very flat route has less than 100 ft (30 m) difference in altitude. In 2011 Wilson Kipsang was only four seconds short of beating the world record. Had the cobblestones not been wet, he would probably have succeeded. Tactically, it is useful to know that the second half is considered faster. Naturally, this also depends on the wind direction

ENTRY FEE From $77 (£46)

THE CITY To a large extent the marathon owes its success to its excellent infrastructure. Whether running through exclusive residential areas, in popular districts, in the woods or along the River Main, the best way to discover the city is by taking part in the marathon.

TIP FOR RUNNERS The programme of fringe events attracts participants with its Relay Marathon and Children's Run. Even the very youngest can take part in the Strewwelpeter Run which is 460 yards (420 m) long. The finish line of the marathon remains open for six hours, so with its flat route the event is accessible to beginners!

CONTACT DETAILS

Frankfurt Marathon
Sonnemannstraße 5
60314 Frankfurt am Main
Germany
Tel.: +49/69/37 00 46 80
Fax: +49/69/370 04 68 11
E-Mail: registration@frankfurt-marathon.com
Internet: www.bmw-frankfurt-marathon.com

Impressions of Osaka: Running under an avenue of gingko trees (top). Sushi is served on the route (center). In this marathon a non-Japanese runner is as exotic as his companion in a manga outfit (bottom).

Osaka Marathon

Making a rainbow together

Japan and the marathon concept go well together. The discipline that is required in training is an inherent trait in the Japanese character. But in the Osaka marathon you will find out how it became a real folk festival event.

In Japan, pure elite runs that take place in city centers on roads cleared of traffic are traditional. But mass sport marathons are a recent manifestation—the first took place in Tokyo in 2007. The Osaka Marathon saw the light in 2012 and by the following year it had already become the second-largest marathon in Japan, attracting over 35,000 runners. Seven million people live in the Osaka region, two million of them in the center. Situated about 250 miles (400 km) south of the capital Tokyo, Osaka grew as a trading city and it is also an economic center. Arriving by plane, it can look as if the pilot is trying to land on the water: in fact, the airport is on an artificial island in the sea, made with tons of sand, since there was no space to build it on the mainland.

There is not much space in the city either. During the marathon, the route is so narrow that there are long sections when it almost impossible to overtake—unless you started at the very front. But throughout the marathon the throng is perfectly managed by the excellent organization. It almost looks as if the marathon only been arranged to prove that the city can organize such a mass event; or to demonstrate how many volunteer helpers they are can muster and control.

Wooden shoes on the asphalt

The friendly helpers stand in line in many places. At the refreshment stations there are almost twice as many helpers as there would be in American or European races of this size. It is very impressive.

But even more impressive is the start near the Osaka Castle. Here the runners form a colorful, crazy band. It is rare to see so many disguises and costumes in a marathon. There are hares with long ears that may be pink, brown or black, countless Supermen and Superwomen, and many exotic creatures from the animal kingdom, including lions and tigers, fish and birds. There are angels and devils and many runners dressed up as the Disney and Manga characters that are so popular in Japan. And there are also runners idressed traditionally as geishas, samurai, karate fighters or judo fighters. There are even runners wearing "getas," the traditional wooden shoes in which the foot rests on an elevated wooden platform. In the past these served to protect against wet, dirt and debris on the streets. Walking in them is wobbly and running is an exercise in extreme skill. It is hard to think of footwear less suitable for running.

The large crowds gathered along the route confirm the popularity of the marathon. Acoustically, the noise they make is modest because the Japanese express their enthusiasm in a subtle manner, albeit a pleasantly appreciative one.

Ginkgos in the autumn light

Most districts through which the marathon route runs look alike, since one skyscraper looks much like another; there is no room for green spaces. An exception is the Mido-Suji Boulevard where runners will enjoy the golden autumn colors of the gingko trees. The route includes most of the architectural landmarks of the city, which was built on a grid pattern so that every 90-degree corner is followed by a straight stretch with a smooth asphalt surface, very easy to run on. The route also takes the runners across several multi-storied bridges. There are refreshment stations every 1.55 miles (2.5 km) offering a wide range of drinks. Halfway through the marathon, runners are given bananas, biscuits and typically Japanese food, while at the 21.74 mile (35 km) mark, rice balls and sushi are served.

"I've learned most about myself and about writing novels through my daily running training."

Haruki Murakami, Japanese writer and marathon runner

INFORMATION

DATE October

PARTICIPANTS 30,000 starters

CHARACTER OF THE ROUTE The Osaka marathon is entertaining in the best sense of the word. Late autumn is a good time to travel because normally there is very little rain. Unfortunately the premiere in 2011 was an exception and it did rain, but the following year the weather was fantastic with extremely pleasant temperatures. Anyone who is planning a running holiday in Japan will discover in Osaka a concentration of Japanese culture, people and urban life in its purest form. As a visiting foreigner he or she will seen as an exotic curiosity.

ENTRY FEE About $125 (£75)

THE CITY A tourist in the center of this large city will not be lost even if he does not speak Japanese. The underground signs in the major stations are all in English and journeys in the crowded trains are a quite an experience. The city center is very stylish, and Kobe and Kyoto are within easy reach.

TIP FOR RUNNERS There are very few suitable running tracks but many international hotels can supply route maps for short but intensive jogging tours round the city.

CONTACT DETAILS
Osaka Association of All Athletics
Osaka Prefectural Government
City of Osaka
Japan
E-Mail: info@osaka-marathon.com
Internet: www.osaka-marathon.com

Venice Marathon
A lot of water and a few lagoon islands

Venice is a magnet, a dream destination for tourists from all over the world. And it also attracts many marathon runners who look forward to the dramatic finish in the floating city in the lagoon.

Runners are tired by the time they arrive at the Grand Canal, but the last miles of the Venice Marathon make up for it. St. Mark's Square is magnificent and the spectators are out in force to welcome the runners.

Only the last section of the Venice Marathon actually runs through Venice, but the marathon is well worth it in spite of that. There are plenty of sights to be seen in the earlier stages. And of course it is an Italian marathon, and Italians adore marathons: the names of Alberto Cova, Orlando Pizzolato, Gianni Poli, Gelindo Bordin and Stefano Baldini are all associated with great marathon victories, with European and World Championship titles. They are stars in Italy and some of them are sure to be attending the start or watching the finish line. And of course the final stage along the Grand Canal to the finish is uniquely spectacular.

A longstanding enthusiasm for marathons
There is an amazingly large number of books on Venice. The image of the city has been enhanced by the numerous films and television productions, from James Bond to Inspector Brunetti, from Don't Look Now to Death in Venice. That is why it is all the more exciting to approach the city on foot. The start is in Strà near the Villa Pisani, a magnificent late baroque villa with over 100 rooms and a somewhat sanguine past, overlooking the Brenta Canal. The runners follow this canal for the first half of the marathon. The route continues to the Villa Malcontenta but the view begins to reveal container ports, industrial warehouses and refineries. The half-marathon point is reached soon afterwards. The next intermediate goal is Mestre.

Into the center of the city
A little after the 20.50 mile (33 km) mark, things become serious—the mainland part of the marathon is coming to an end. The runners now cross the bridge, the Ponte della Libertà, into Venice. It is Venice's lifeline and therefore not entirely closed off to traffic. It is a tough challenge for the runners to face at this point because the bridge is 2.48 miles (4 km) long. Progress is slow even with a tailwind and the skyline of Venice seems to approach desperately slowly. But somehow

the runners make it. The "Grand Finale" is close now as they reaching Giudecca Canale: the last 1.86 miles (3 km) run through the very heart of Venice.

Now the route is up a wooden ramp over one of Venice's numerous bridges. The steps are steep so the marathon organizers have covered them with wooden boards to make a ramp that is easier to cross. In fact there are 14 bridges to cross. And of course the sidewalks that link these bridges are becoming increasingly narrow: this is Venice, after all. Now the first gondolier appears, ironically offering his services to the runners. The sidewalk comes to an end at the Punta della Dogana, the Customs Point, where the Grand Canal and Canale della Giudecca flow together.

Normally you can go no further from here, except by gondola, water-taxi or ferry.

But for the marathon the organizers have built a temporary pontoon bridge over the Grand Canal that joins up with the district of San Marco. The spire of the campanile on the Piazza San Marco shows the way to go. The marathon route runs in and out of the famous Piazza San Marco with the Doges' Palace and the Basilica; then it continues to the east and over ramps, bridges and boards towards the finish on the Riva dei Sette Martiri.

Here the route is wide enough again for the crowds of spectators who enthusiastically applaud the runners at the finish.

"Running,
I do not think."
Dieter Baumann

INFORMATION

DATE October

PARTICIPANTS 6,000 starters

CHARACTER OF THE ROUTE The route is considered fast - at least if the wind comes/blows mostly from behind. Otherwise you must adapt to the conditions; the last 1.86 miles (3 km) take the runners into the real Venice as we see it in films, magazines and books. The Venice Marathon is the third-largest in Italy and has a large local participation.

ENTRY FEE About $100 (£60)

THE CITY Venice with its bridges, gondolas and St. Mark's Square - this picture is confirmed by the marathon, although only towards the end. Nevertheless the marathon gives an interesting perspective because the runners are discovering the city as few tourists have seen and experienced it.

TIP FOR RUNNERS Those who are staying in Venice itself should definitely go for a run in the early morning because the city becomes too crowded later and the streets too congested. It is best to prepare themselves and run a short circuit several times.

CONTACT DETAILS

A.S.D. Venicemarathon Club
Via Linghindal, 5/5
30172 Venice
ITALY
Tel: +39 041/532 1871
Fax: +39 041/532 1879
Italy
E-Mail: info@venicemarathon.it
Internet: www.venicemarathon.it

Functional clothing can provide good protection against dry cold (top and bottom). The musk oxen (center) are better protected with a thick coat of fur.

Polar Circle Marathon
The coolest marathon on earth

The Polar Circle Marathon takes the runners over glaciers and across the Greenland tundra, a forbidding landscape. Provided you have good equipment, you are sure to have an unforgettable running experience. The cold temperatures are compensated for by the warm and friendly atmosphere among the runners.

The Eskimos have known it for a long time. Snow is not just white. Its frozen splendor displays a wide range of shades of white: whites ranging from soft to hard, from bright to dark, from pale to bold. So the Eskimos have many names for it. And here, at the Polar Circle Marathon, the runners can understand why. In the morning as they make their way to the start in the all-wheel drive bus, they will have passed dozens of shades of white. And the naked ice that is seen protruding from the glacier looks dark and deep. The ice here is at least 8,000 years old and as hard as concrete.

Snow like quicksand
In the Polar Circle Marathon, ice and snow play a major part. "Many years you will find it very difficult without spikes," Lars Fyhr, the race organizer warns. And the runners realize very soon after the start how right he was to say this: the going is quite easy for the first 1.24 miles (2 km) but then it is increasingly uphill and ever steeper. The fresh snow feels a little like quicksand and with every footstep you lose a little of your strength in the dry crystals.

Suddenly there a short very steep downslope. Beneath the powdery snow is solid ice. The runners are now on the Russell glacier. The steel pins of the spikes hook into the ice and stop the runners from slipping. It is a loop 1.86 mile (3 km) long up the glacier that is reached soon after sunrise.

The sun rises slowly, very slowly as if it had attuned itself to the frozen slowness of nature. It is completely flat above the horizon, its light is filtered by thin clouds. And it illuminates the snow and ice with an indescribable light: red, orange, yellow, blue, grey and green all merging into each other. The shadows are faint and low. The runners in the distance are like ice statues. The could even be mistaken for an expedition of arctic explorers. Their faces are all wrapped up. Many wear goggles, not against the light

but against the cold. They also put a special cream on their face for the same reason. The small field of runners follow each like a string of loosely strung pearls. No one overtakes, everyone is happy to follow the track that the runner in front has made slightly deeper. Often the runners sink as much as 1 ft (30 cm) into the snowdrifts. Some wear gaiters to prevent the snow from getting into their running shoes.

The humidity in the air is very low and the snow is very dry in the below-freezing temperatures so it is easy to tap off one's clothes. There are track marshals at two places on the glacier to warn the runners about the slippery, bare ice. The layer of ice is about 8 in (20 cm) thick and it looks clear and clean, dark and deep. Fascination has the upper hand over the slightly uncomfortable feeling that this inhospitable, lifeless place arouses in everyone.

From the glacier to the tundra

The "runners" trudge slowly along, walking carefully, marveling at their surroundings, panting and staring at the ice. The sun rises inch by inch above the horizon: like the runners, it is certainly in no hurry. The route across the Russell Glacier describes

The steep ascent up the glacier moraine in the early morning sun (top), with glaciers in the background. A wit has added an ironic notice to the 7 km marker (above).

The route leads over the Russell Glacier (above) and is marked with flags; or just follow the tracks of the person in front. The small field of competitors quickly becomes spaced out (center and bottom).

a loop. The organizers have set up an additional refreshment point after 3.1 miles (5 km) where runners can enjoy a warm drink. Also a pair of dry shoes and equipment can be kept here. This is an understandable precaution: most runners use up almost a quarter of their running time in this first, spectacular part of the marathon. Although it is only 5°F (-15°C)—in valleys it is much colder—the participants do not feel cold in the dry air when they run, at least not physically. The air you breath in and out is cold. The lenses of the goggles do not steam up, they ice up.

After leaving the glacier, the route takes the runners into the tundra. The tracks are deserted. The uneven trail on which only off-road vehicle can move winds its way across 21.74 miles (35 km) to the finish in Kangerlussuaq, a group of huts in the west of Greenland dating from the 1940s when the American built a military airfield there. Now it is used as a civil airport. Consisting mainly of huts housing the 500 inhabitants who are connected in some way with the airfield, the village is north of the Arctic Circle. The climate here is extremely stable and is covered in ice six months of the year. Admittedly it gets cold in winter but there is relatively little snow. "We almost never have to cancel flights at any time of the year," Jörgen Larsen of the Greenland Tourist Office explains. "In fact you can always land here."

Very soon the runners realize that the track is now only covered with a thin layer of snow. Now their

shoes now crunch very softly in the snow again. On the slopes of Mount Sugar Loaf musk oxen can be seen, very warm in their thick, shaggy coat. Encounters with other runners are rare. Some of them would later explain that they had run the whole marathon completely on their own. That too is quite a unique experience. Some runners will be slower, others faster on the uphill—and on downhill slopes, only a very few run together. When they encounter each other either at refreshment points or when overtaking, they exchange of few encouraging words, after which they continue on their own enjoying the stillness around them.

You don't choose Greenland because of the spectators. The only sound the runners hear is the sound of their own footsteps. The very soft crunching. Often it is only a very light creaking, caused by the pressure of the shoes on the loose powdery snow. And sometimes it is the sound of scraping when the spikes on the soles hook into the ice of the Russell Glacier. Or it may be the sound of one's own breathing, the rustling of clothes. Otherwise there is complete silence. No wind, no birds, only a couple of runners in the distance.

Sauna in sight

After a long, energy-sapping climb, the valley widens at the 12.42 mile (20 km) mark. A third of the runners have opted for the half-marathon and they are cold but happy as they climb into the well-heated buses parked along the road. Until this point the route had wound its way in a succession of up and down stretches, first to the right and then the left. Now is more even. Kangerlussuaq, the finish, is some 660 ft (200 m) below the start at Point 660, so

from now on it is all gently downhill. Most marathon runners are faster on the second half because of the easier terrain and soon they arrive at the finish in Kangerlussuaq where a couple of spectators and the sauna are waiting.

The important thing about this marathon is the route itself. Nature itself is the attraction because there is hardly anything else along the route—apart from a useless piste basher and the wreckage of military plane that crashed over twenty years ago that the runners barely even notice. And equally unnoticed is the curious golf course at the 23.61 mile (38 km) mark that must be the northermost 18-hole golf course in the world. But not surprisingly the runners have other things on their mind!

"Running has given me an idea of the maximum freedom that a person can have."

Sir Roger Bannister

INFORMATION

DATE October (date provisional)

PARTICIPANTS About 100 starters

CHARACTER OF THE ROUTE The Polar Circle marathon is a real challenge but also a unique experience. Admittedly the climate in this fjord landscape is reliable, but it is cold... The temperature can be as high as 50°F (10°C) or as low as -4°F (-20°C). Participation in this marathon or half-marathon is only possible by booking a complete package. The experience is incomparable.

ENTRY FEE From $385 (£230)

THE REGION Greenland is an increasingly popular travel destination throughout the year. In summer, the region attracts ramblers and in winter holidaymakers are offered a wide range of snow-related activities, ranging from dog-sled rides to walking in the snow with snow shoes.

TIP FOR RUNNERS Running conditions depend very much on the time of the day and the weather on that day; it is best to ask ask the locals about the weather conditions and run when there is little wind because the cold will be more bearable. After two days you will have become accustomed to the temperatures.

CONTACT DETAILS

Polar Circle Marathon
Tøndergade 16
1752 Kopenhagen V
Denmark
Tel: +45/3698 9898
Fax: +45/3698 9899
E-Mail: info@adventure-marathon.com
Internet: www.polar-circle-marathon.com

New York Marathon

Others do it smaller

New York not only has the tallest skyscrapers, the most popular parks and the most famous museums in the world. This creative chaos of the different districts, nations and civilizations produces one of the most spectacular marathon events. The run symbolizes how this city has made a virtue of its seemingly irreconcilable contrasts.

The best way to get a taste of the whole of New York in about four to five hours is to take part in the New York Marathon. Along the way there are always new perspectives.

When, as a runner, you cross the area from Ford Wadsworth to the start of the New York marathon and look around absorbing the atmosphere, you become aware that there is something unusual in the air. This is more than the normal pre-race nerves. The runners are from all over the world and they are all speaking different languages. Loud rock music is being played in the background; live bands are playing on two stages and the atmosphere is that of an open-air music festival. Some of the runners are dancing while others are lounging around on the grass. Hot tea and biscuits are on offer. There is a strong smell of muscle oil.

Further on the Verrazano Narrows Bridge is closed to traffic and waiting for the runners. At 9:45 the first runners cross the bridge on both its levels and make their way towards Brooklyn. In the distance they can distinguish the Manhattan skyline, shrouded in a light haze. After all the runners have gathered on the starting line, the US national anthem The Star-Spangled Banner, is sung. Then after the starting signal, Frank Sinatra's "New York, New York," is played on the loudspeaker. The words about this unique city really touch the runners and many sing along with it: "If I can make it there, I'll make it anywhere." There are 40,000 colorful dots making indescribable panoramic picture as they cross the Verrazano Narrows Bridge, one of the longest steel suspension bridges in the world.

A connecting route
The marathon starts on Staten Island and makes its way towards Central Park. It is like a little tour round the world and at the same time a discovery of the city and the marathon. New York heralded a new era when in 1976 it was decided that the marathon should take place in the heart of the city. Before then, from 1970, it had been run on a repeating circuit in Central Park.

It was the founder and ideas man Fred Lebow—who died in 1994—who organized the New York City marathon so that it went through the five boroughs. He was assisted by George Hirsch who remembers the bold plan: "We had planned the run as a gala with a two-year cycle. The city was almost bankrupt at the time. And we went to see the then mayor and submitted our idea to him—arguing that the marathon would lift the mood in the city. We could not know if the race would be popular. But anyway the race was so successful that it took place every year and united the whole city."

The route runs through the five boroughs—each one as distinctive as a capital in its own right—emphasizing the size of New York as well as the length of the marathon. Like a necklace stringing together pearls of different colors, the marathon strings together the five boroughs: from the start on Staten Island across Brooklyn, Queens, the Bronx and finally Manhattan. Districts that as different from each other as the five fingers of a hand, yet somehow they form a geographic community together.

At the same time the marathon unites these opposites. And that is a success reaching far beyond the running aspects

Immediately after the start the Verrazano Narrows Bridge is crossed, on both the upper level (above), and on the lower level beneath it.

The finish in Central Park fulfils a long-held dream for many runners. many runners a long-held dream—whether it be to cross the finish line first, just to be involved, or to have achieved good performance.

of the event. New York has been a pioneer in many things. Not just that in 1976 it hosted the first city marathon, an example that was then followed by cities including Stockholm, Paris, Berlin, London and Rotterdam. The New York marathon has always allowed women to take part—from the very beginning. And the New York Marathon has also showed how marathons could attract tourists.

Manhattan—so near and yet so far
But back to the route. In the heat of the start, most runners do not realize that they have made an elevation gain of 165 ft (50 m) up to the Verrazano Narrows Bridge in just 1 mile (1.6 km). It is partly the magnificent view of Manhattan that has taken their mind off this aspect. There are no spectators to speak of on the bridge. They are waiting after the bridge like a reception committee. The marathon route follows Fourth Avenue in Brooklyn for 4.97 miles (8 km), in a dead straight line. Here again the route is thickly lined with spectators. And at each block a band is playing some kind of music—brash, country, hip-hop and often such good rock music you should really pay extra admission fee for it.

Not surprisingly, Brooklyn has become one of the trendiest districts in New York. There was a time when it was bigger and more important than Manhattan and now it is back in the limelight. The side streets are lined with fashionable bars and some of the best art galleries in the city. A tip: anyone running this marathon should first read up about the culture and history of each

borough. Like the section reached after about an hour: Williamsburg, where the streets on Sunday morning are filled with marathon runners, orthodox Jews and funky-looking people.

Shortly before the Pulaski Bridge, the runners reach the half-marathon mark. It's a good time to listen to your inner voice and decide whether the glass is still half full or already half empty. The Pulaski Bridge is a hotspot for photographers because the view from here across the East River towards the Manhattan skyline is magnificent, so much so that some runners even stop and take pictures. After the bridge the runners reach Queens, a borough with over two million people from 150 countries. Again like a city within a city. Again with a different character and atmosphere contributing to the diversity of the melting pot that is New York.

A short rest during the race
After about 15.5 miles (25 km), the runners cross the Queensboro Bridge and there is an impressive silence for a few minutes. You hear nothing except for the sound of running shoes on the asphalt. Spectators are not allowed on the bridge on which—as well as the marathon runners today—the subway trains run. Even photographers need special permission. The runners are among themselves. A rare, almost reflective moment in the New York Marathon.

But then, as soon as you get off the bridge there is a sharp left turn: the curtain rises! Welcome to Manhattan! Spectators have already taken up their position before the runners arrive, clustered in several rows behind each other so as to get the best view of the show. The runners turn here on the Upper East Side into First Avenue. The eight-lane avenue has been completely closed to traffic for the runners who can see straight ahead for miles towards the Bronx, with spectators clustered all along the route. Many countries have been assigned their fan mile here.

The runners continue along First Avenue for about 3.72 miles (6 km), cheered on by countless excited spectators, but it is important to keep an eye on the road because there are many potholes that have caused many a runner to stumble or fall. After some 19.88 miles (32 km) the runners reach the Willis Avenue Bridge across the Harlem River. Here they make a short detour through the Bronx. This is one of the loudest sections of the route and the mood is extremely boisterous.

From the Bronx the route goes back towards Manhattan. Spectators are lining the route from Fifth Avenue to Central Park. When the runners enter the park with its gold-yellow autumn colors, many will imagine they have reached the finish: but the route continues for a few more miles along the park, round the bottom and then a few yards north again. There's a climb that is very hard on the tired marathon legs. Even the last 550 yards (500 m) are slightly uphill: but anyone who succeeds here will succeed everywhere.

"I'm never going to run this again."

Grete Waitz (Norwegian), after the first of his nine wins in New York

INFORMATION

DATE First Sunday in November

PARTICIPANTS About 40,000 starters

CHARACTER OF THE ROUTE Of the 600 marathons in the U.S., the New York Marathon is the most spectacular. The route has it all. The point-to-point marathon course is undulating and has through the crossings of the bridge several meters up on .

ENTRY FEE About $550 (£325)

THE CITY There is no single New York. Each neighborhood has its own culture and its own character, arising from the history of its inhabitants and the dynamics of a city that never sleeps.

TIP FOR RUNNERS Demand for registration far exceeds the number of places in the marathon, so runners are chosen by lottery. A way of guaranteeing entry is to run for Team for Kids, which requires an individual commitment of $2,500 (1,500) or more. Details are on the organizer's website.

CONTACT DETAILS
New York Road Runners
9 E 89th Street
New York, NY 10128
United States of America
Tel.: +1/855/5MY NYRR
E-Mail: mynyrr@nyrr.org
Internet: www.tcsnycmarathon.org

Winter

Marathon runs in the winter have a charm of their own. The cold air is much clearer and cleaner. The difficulties are different ones. But many runners deal better with the cold than with the heat. The best thermal power station when running is undoubtedly the body and running makes it work. The crunching and creaking of the snow under one's running shoes under a blue sky on a clear winter's day is pure pleasure.

Running always lifts the spirits, whether the weather is hot or cold.

The marathon of modern times started in 1896, in the city of Marathon, north of Athens. Today the start is still there (top) while the finish is in the historic Olympic Stadium in Athens (bottom).

Athens Marathon

Beginnings and origins

Here the legend was born. Athens has this unique advantage over all other marathons. The first Olympic Games of modern times were held in Athens in 1896, and the first marathon was part of them.

The place is called Marathon. And where could one start a marathon, if not there,? It was there that it all began and it is there that it still starts today. As it did in 1896, the Athens Marathon still starts in the place to the north-east of Athens that gave its name to the sport. The route takes the runners to the most traditional of finishes: the white marble Panathenaiko Stadium constructed for the 1896 Olympic Games. A more symbolic place does not exist.

Legend or not? No matter!

But now to the legend. In the Battle of Marathon in 490 BC, the Greeks defeated the superior power of the Persians. The legend is that the Greek messenger Pheidippides ran from Marathon to Athens bringing the news of the victory: "We have won." Those were his last words. Then he collapsed and died. It may be true or it may be a legend; either way, it adds a touch of heroism to the sporting discipline of the marathon. But there is one thing that those

planning a start in Marathon should know. It is a tough route with some serious climbs. And although in some years there is rain and fog, it can become very hot during the race.

The first marathon winner in 1896 was Spyridon Louis who, as the only Greek gold medal winner, became a national hero. He too found it very hot and is said to have asked for wine during the race—wine being the ancient form of sports drink. Spyridon Louis was one of seventeen participants, thirteen from Greece and four from other countries, running on the dirt roads and rough cobblestones.

He arrived at the stadium in the lead to a rapturous reception, being accompanied on the final lap by the two Greek princes, Crown Prince Constantine and Prince George. He was congratulated by the King himself.

In the footsteps of Spyridon Louis

Nowadays the heat often glimmers above the wide arterial roads of the route. The Japanese writer Haruki

144

Murakami, author of *What I Talk About When I Talk About Running*, chose the Athens Marathon for his first marathon (he has now taken part in more than twenty marathons). He suffered dreadfully in the summer smog, the Mediterranean heat and hilliness of the route. The middle part of the route is well-know its long, debilitating climb.

So why take part in the Athens Marathon? Amby Burfoot, winner of the 1968 Boston Marathon and one of the most accomplished running journalists, has the answer. He took part in the Athens Marathon in 2010, the year in which the 2500th anniversary of the Battle of Marathon was being celebrated. "I was running in the footsteps of the legendary Pheidippides and the real Spyridon Louis." Burfoot makes this comparison: "For a long-distance runner the Athens Marathon touches your soul in the same way that Jerusalem or Mecca do in the case of religious pilgrims." Anyone who takes part in the Athens Marathon will experience a similar emotion, particularly at the start and finish. The IAAF has awarded it Gold Label Road Race certification.

The runner Hans Pertsch describes his finish as follows: "The finish could not be more moving. Instead of extravagant light shows and fireworks, the spectators cheer the runners as they enter the historic Olympic Stadium in Athens. Such moisture as the body still has now flows down the runners' cheeks in the form of tears."

> *"Dedicate your next marathon to someone special."*
>
> Joe Henderson

INFORMATION

DATE November

PARTICIPANTS About 7,000 starters

CHARACTER OF THE ROUTE The race starts in the village of Marathon at 9 a.m. by which time the temperature may already be 64°F (18 C). The city circuit goes round the burial mound of the Athenians who fell in the Battle of Marathon. The first quarter of the route is flat. But then the runners face some uphill stretches. And just as the runners arrive at the critical threshold of 19.88 miles (32 km) near Agia Paraskevi, they reach the highest point of the route, 790 ft (240 m) above sea level. Then it is all downhill to the finish in the Panathinaiko Stadium in Athens.

ENTRY FEE From $85 (£50)

THE CITY Athens with its superb Acropolis and other classical sites has the same appeal as the marathon: both are rich in history and fascinating mythology.

TIP FOR RUNNERS Several tour operators specializing in running events offer packages including visits to some of the ancient sites.

CONTACT DETAILS
SEGAS (Hellenic Athletics Federation)
Marathon Office
137 Syngrou Avenue
171 21 Nea Smirni, Athena
Greece
Tel.: +30/210/933 11 13 oder
+30/210/931 58 86
Fax: +30/210/933 11 52
E-Mail: info@athensclassicmarathon.gr
Internet: www.athensclassicmarathon.gr

All the ingredients for a delightful atmosphere. The run is enhanced by the glittering sea, the sandy beaches, the palm trees on the promenade (top and center), and of course the finish on La Croisette in Cannes (bottom).

Nice-Cannes Marathon
Yes we Cannes. It's very Nice.

Sun, sea and palm trees: the course of the Marathon des Alpes Maritimes Nice-Cannes runs for 26.2 miles (42.195) km runs along the coast through a uniquely beautiful part of the French Riviera. The finish is on La Croisette in Cannes in front of the glamorous Carlton Hotel.

Nice is effectively the capital of the French Riviera and has been so for a long time. The start is on the Promenade des Anglais, which is so-called because of the many British visitors who spent the winter there in the 19th century: it was already a favored tourist destination.

What makes Nice so unique? It is the combination of the magnificent landscape with the Alps in the background with the agreeable Mediterranean climate. Then there is the amazing play of light: the blazing sun emphasizes the turquoise blue of the sea and the green of the palm trees. The painter Henri Matisse fell in love with this view and spent most of his life here. Suffering from bronchitis, he had been advised by his doctor to spend time in Nice.

The Marathon des Alpes-Maritimes Nice-Cannes, or the Nice Marathon for short, takes place in very exclusive surroundings. The start of the race is as select as the finish on the Boulevard de la Croisette in Cannes.

Panorama for a Sunday walk
When it was held for the first time in 2008, the Nice Marathon was already the second-largest in France, after Paris. The runners had apparently been waiting for such race along the Mediterranean. Apart from Paris, there is no other big-city marathon in France—perhaps reflecting the preferences on the French running scene. There are many trail-running events that attract large numbers of runners. While the Toulouse Marathon attracted about 4,000 runners, in the same weekend 8,000 runners took part in the Festival des Templiers trail event. Even with the much longer distance of the Ultra-Trail du Mont Blanc, one of the most challenging trail events, 4,000 runners took part.

Compared to that ultramarathon, the Marathon des Alpes-Maritimes is a like a Sunday walk—or at least the scenery is. The route passes through many tourist resorts: Saint-Laurent-du-Var, Cagnes-sur-Mer, Villeneuve-Loubet, Antibes, Juan-Les-pins and Vallauris. All lovers of France will find their mouths watering at the sound of these names, a feeling no doubt shared by the 11,000 participants.

Enthusiastic reception

The start of the race is on the Promenade des Anglais, which is completely closed to traffic. It is November and runners who have come from colder climes will enjoy the pleasantly mild temperatures, warm enough to wear shorts. The runners are happy. First they pass the Hotel Negresco, an elegant building dating from the Belle Époque. Meanwhile the atmosphere is warming up. The marathon is generously supported by the localities it passes through and runners are encouraged on their way by the cheering crowds.

This is also true of the grand finish. Cannes is reached after 24.85 miles (40 km). And as with the Tour de France, numerous spectators have gathered on La Croisette where the atmosphere is now electric. But unlike in the bicycle race, here all the competitors are cheered, even those who do not finish amongst the leaders. The Hotel Carlton is the place to see and be seen, while in the marathon, the motto is to run and be seen.

"The true runner is a very fortunate person. He has found something in him that is just perfect."

George Sheehan

INFORMATION

DATE November

PARTICIPANTS About 11,000 starters

CHARACTER OF THE ROUTE The route winds its way up and down along the coast. Near Cap d'Antibes and Golfe Juan the runners will encounter short, steep climbs. One of the most beautiful sections of the route is in the historic town of Antibes, a little over halfway through the marathon. Sometimes runners will be able to see the snow-covered Alpine peaks on one side and the white crests of the waves of the Mediterranean on the other.

ENTRY FEE Ab 45 Euro

THE REGION The Côte d'Azur is one of the most popular vacation regions in France and November is a perfect month for visiting. It is still pleasantly warm but no longer too hot. These are perfect conditions for tourists and marathon runners alike.

Another bonus is that prices will have dropped a little because it is the low season.

TIP FOR RUNNERS Runners will find some delightful tracks and footpaths with panoramic views of the Alpes Maritimes which are quite close to Nice. Here everyone will find something to their taste.

CONTACT DETAILS

Azur Sport Organisation
1 Boulevard Maître Maurice Slama
Nice premium
06200 Nice
France
Tel. +33/ 04 93 26 19 12
E-Mail: info@azur-sport.org
Internet: www.marathon06.com

The start of the marathon takes place early in the morning in Orchard Road, which becomes very busy with shoppers later in the day. The runners include carnival characters and many others who prefer to take things slowly.

Singapore Marathon

Brave the pain. Celebrate after!

Singapore is a thrilling place. It is a microcosm of different cultures and civilizations ready to be discovered. The marathon too has its own rules, reflecting Singapore's comprehensive network of laws and regulations.

Singapore is a truly fascinating place. This small country has undergone a transformation equaled by few other regions in the world. It is in fact only a small island (or group of islands) at the south-eastern corner of the Asian continent. But now it is one of the four "tiger economies" that has shown its claws and it has secured a large slice of the international financial cake. The official name of the Singapore marathon is the Standard Chartered Singapore Marathon.

Fifty years ago, before Singapore became independent, no one could have anticipated such a thing. It has transformed itself into an economic power where large international multi-corporate enterprises have established offices, where old British colonial-style buildings rub shoulders with gigantic skyscrapers, where Chinatown and Little India exist next to each other. There are four official languages and many others used in this Asian melting-pot that has one of the highest population densities in the world. As a tourist, you need a while to get even a vague idea of the place. And as soon as you have done so, you may already have to leave.

A greenhouse climate

How did the marathon come about? Singapore has hosted running events for many years and the marathon was first held here in the 1980s. Since then it has evolved and developed, and now over 15,000 runners take part. There are also a half-marathon, relay races, school races and fitness races so that in all some 60,000 people take part in the events.

There are still comparatively few American participants, which in view of flight time of nearly 24 hours is not surprising. And then there is also the climate: the temperature is at least 77°F (25°C) and it often rises well above 86°F (30°C), combined an extremely high air humidity which tends to be about 80 to

90 percent throughout the year. December is therefore the best month for a marathon because it is the coolest month of the year. It also tends to rains a lot then but this can be refreshing, and the sun will soon shine again.

Strictly organized and regulated

As a marathon runner you soon form an impression of the city and its customs—such as having to pick up your starting number within a certain time-frame. Organization and planning are paramount in Singapore and naturally this also applies to the marathon—down to the enthusiasm that is generated in the population. The marathon starts early, at 5 a.m., in Orchard Road, one of the most popular shopping streets in the city. It should also be mentioned that Singapore has some very strict laws and regulations. Littering is heavily fined and chewing gum sales are prohibited, although gum can be chewed provided it is properly disposed of. You should not be put off by this but remain relaxed because the marathon too is a relaxed affair.

No other big-city marathon is as slow as the Singapore marathon because the heat and humidity reduce the pace considerably. The mid-field completes the race in about 6 hours. And this in itself adds a very special dimension to the marathon experience, in other words you discover slowness—and so you also discover faces of Singapore that no other tourist will.

*"Run slowly.
Run daily.
Don't be greedy.
Drink in moderation.*

Ernst van Aaken

INFORMATION

DATE December

PARTICIPANTS About 15,000 starters

CHARACTER OF THE ROUTE This is an excellently organized running event closely integrated with the life of the city. The running ambition of participants is remarkably easy. The marathon is mainly influenced by the sultry warm climate so it is necessary to be prepared for that.

ENTRY FEE $60 (£35)

THE CITY The island of Singapore is often visited as a stopover on the way to more distant destinations and indeed a short visit is well worthwhile. In spite of its high-density development and crowds everywhere the financial metropolis has some pleasant green corners—although they are sometimes found on the roof of a skyscraper.

TIP FOR RUNNERS Singapore is one of the most densely populated cities in the world. It is not easy to train by running through the city so it makes better sense for travelers to run on the treadmill at the gym or at the hotel. Outside, it is often simply too humid during the day, as well as too crowded. An alternative is to run in the evenings or at night when it is cooler .

CONTACT DETAILS
Spectrum Worldwide Events (Singapore) Pte. Ltd.
221 Henderson Road 01–02,
Henderson Building
Singapore 159557
Tel. +65/66 43 91 91
E-Mail: info@marathonsingapore.com
Internet: www.marathonsingapore.com

Running shoes: the perfect shoe does not exist. Every runner must find the model that is best.

Marathon equipment
From shoes to scarves

One of great advantages of running is its amazing flexibility. You can run anywhere. You do not need a sports center, a partner, a timetable or a venue. And you can fit all your equipment in your hand luggage. Runners need just a few things—but these are vitally important.

In normal weather, a runner will need running shoes and socks, trousers, a top and, in the case of women, a sports bra. That is all a runner needs, although the list of available equipment for runners can easily reach fifty. Most of these are not needed for running a marathon. Instead marathon runners should concentrate on the essentials. Running light is the motto, with as little ballast as possible. The vital question is: what do you need to complete a marathon? A smartphone for instance is not on the list of equipment—although half the American runners in the New York Marathon seem to disagree with this.

Running shoes
The choice of running shoes is mostly dictated by the runner's preference: they will be shoes that have been sufficiently tested in training and that have also proved satisfactory over long distances. The commonest problem that marathon

runners encounter is that their shoes are too small. Running shoes need to be larger than ordinary sports shoes; the foot must have sufficient space in the toe area—especially for a marathon. You can easily check this with the "thumb rule." For this, the laces must be carefully tied; then stand up with your weight distributed equally on both feet: there should still be the width of a thumb in front of the longest toe. (Note that the longest toe is not necessarily the longest toe—it is often the second toe.) The reason for this extra room is that the feet spread out when you run. This is partly caused by the weight load. In the "take-off phase," the foot is burdened with at least twice the body weight. As a result the toes dig in—the gripping reflex. That is why you need extra space in the toe area.

Very few runners will need special competition shoes; these are only worthwhile for ambitious runners with a target time of under 3 hours. The best shoes are a good compromise between damping, stability and lightness. During a marathon—which the average runner will take over 4 hours to complete—the muscles get tired. This is when runners will benefit from the damping and support of good running shoes.

Important: there are no standard criteria for "damping" and "stability" so they must be matched to each runner individually. They will vary according to gender, weight, style of running as well as on the external temperature, because many midsoles are made

of synthetic materials that harden in the cold. By way of comparison: a bus needs different tires and shock absorbers from a small car. It is the same with runners—a man of 220 lb (100 kg) pounding the marathon track, needs different shoes from a Kenyan of 110 lb (50 kg) flying across it. In addition, the weight of the shoe itself is also important because it is a dead weight that must be accelerated. The good news is that modern trainers have become so light that they do not feel like a heavy weight on your feet.

Running clothes
The kind of clothes a runner wears when running depends on numerous individual factors. Ignoring the fashion aspects, the perception of heat and cold as well as perspiration varies from person to person. This is affected by gender, training level, muscle mass, circulation and habit. The most frequent mistake made by

runners is that they are too warmly dressed. What they are not allowing for is that when they run the body becomes a thermal power station. The energy output is multiplied. The burning of calories increases to about 10 kcal per 2.2 lb (10 kcal per kg) of weight. This generates first body heat and then energy to enable movement. The body starts to sweat. That is why it needs less heat protection; it is more important that clothing should conduct away the moisture released.

Rule 1: Do not dress too warmly for a marathon but dress in such a way that you are shivering slightly at the start. As a rule of thumb: choose your clothes as if the outdoor temperature was 18°F (10°C) warmer than it is.

Rule 2: Keep the body as dry as possible and wear functional clothes that absorb or convey moisture. Cotton soaks up moisture while artificial fibers absorb no moisture

Favorite shoes. Runners must test their shoes thoroughly before using them in a marathon.

The most important signals for a runner come from the body. A heart-rate monitor can also help.

to speak of. But the construction of the weave is such that the moisture is conveyed to the outside of the clothes where it can evaporate. This helps to regulate body warmth and is therefore a decisive factor in the runner's performance.

Rule 3: The clothes must fit snugly. This means that the trousers and top must be skintight. In this way the clothes function better, they rub less on the skin and they trouble the runner less because they not flap round the body. As far as the socks are concerned: unlike running shoes, running socks must fit the foot tightly.

Running accessories
Everything that is carried on the body while running is ballast. This is why it is important to keep it to a minimum. As pointed out earlier, a smartphone is not necessary when running. The time can be measured with a thin wristwatch. A basic rule is never to try anything in a marathon that you have not already tried on a long run. And that includes not only the running shoes and clothes but also a drink strap, cap and gloves.

General tips
Forward planning is particularly necessary when travelling to marathons in different climate zones. The equipment must always be adapted to the running conditions. In the Tahiti Marathon, for instance, sun protection will be needed while in the North Pole Marathon a cryoprotectant mask will be required, and in desert marathons a snake-bite antidote should be carried.

The complete marathon outfit must be tested in advance on long training runs, as should any cold protection creams or creams to soothe chafing or (for men) plasters to protect the nipples.

Frequently small accessories can be quite useful, such as oversleeves and running gloves. If you can prevent the hands and arms from getting cold, this will have a positive effect on the warmth of the entire body. For the same reason it is a good idea to wear a hat or a running cap if weather conditions require it.

A rather banal problem: how do you make sure that your laces will not get undone? The answer lies in using the right knot. Many runners tie their laces rather carelessly or with the knot and bow in the same direction. In fact the knot and bow should be tied in the opposite direction. Also the laces must not be too long. The laces should be rather flat, like tagliatelle, not round like spaghetti. Flat laces have a larger rubbing surface and therefore the knot and bow will hold better. They should also be slightly stretchy. Important: the laces should exert equal pressure on the flat part of the upper surface of the foot. Only then will the shoes fit well and the laces not get undone.

To sum up, everything that you carry, wear, eat or take with you on the marathon must have thoroughly tested beforehand.

Marathon runners must pay close attention to every detail of their equipment. This certainly applies to lacing the running shoes. The marathon itself is no time for experiment, since by then everything must be a matter of routine.

On the island of Moorea (top), about half-an-hour's boat ride away from the neighboring island of Tahiti, a running dream comes true. The route runs past palm trees and along the white sand beaches (center). After the marathon there is dancing (bottom).

Tahiti-Moorea Marathon
The finish at the blue lagoon

The Tahiti-Moorea Marathon is as relaxing as it is beguiling. In spite of the challenge and heat associated with it, the runners will soak up the fascinating South Sea atmosphere. It takes place on Tahiti's neighboring island of Moorea where the runners will delight in the exotic surroundings, enjoying freshly picked pineapple, coconuts or raw fish.

The race is an experience for the senses. The start is early, long before sunrise, so as to take advantage of the cool of the night. The leafy canopy of the tall coconut trees stands out against the bright starry sky and throws shadows on the asphalt that still retains the warmth of the previous' day's sun. Just a few minutes after the start the initial excitement has abated and calm has returned. Soon the small field of marathon and half-marathon runners is strung out like a pearl necklace. Besides the distant sounds from the tropical forest, the runners can hear the occasional despondent cock crowing. Before long these sounds fade away and the only sound is the noise of running shoes on the asphalt.

Slowly, leisurely, the dawn is approaching and a light breeze refreshes the runners. The sweet fragrance of bougainvilleas envelop the runners. Further on gardenia flowers can be seen. The Tahitians— and the tourists—love wearing these gardenias behind the ear: behind the left ear, if you are single, behind the right one if you are married. But not everyone is particular about this.

Runners may be admired in Tahiti, but they are not worshipped; rather they are mocked a bit. "Running? In this heat?" most Tahitians ask themselves. It is something tourists do. The few locals who take part will find themselves in the lists of results for years. Once a runner, always a runner.

Flowers at the refreshment stand
Except for a few short sections, the route winds it way along the coast. Although the coastal road has not been blocked to traffic there is very little of it and what there is is mostly in the villages. The refreshment stands are a highlight in their own right. The most beautiful one is awarded a prize: to decide the winner a specially appointed jury drives along the entire route and judges the stands, all of

which are beautifully decorated with flowers, together with volunteer helpers dressed in the local costume.

Target times are a side issue, no one is interested. With a temperature of 89.6°F (32°C) in the shade, the runners drag themselves one after the other across the finish line, most of them undaunted, heat-resistant tourists. By 7 a.m. the sun is already burning fiercely. Only the occasional breadfruit tree, coconut palm or fragrant gardenia shrubs provide a little shade at times.

The final sprint? Not really, the "finishing straight" is in the soft sand of Tamae Beach, right on the sea, where the finish banner is hung up between two palm trees. Here any sprinting ambitions will immediately get stuck in the sand. So after crossing the finish line, the runners just slip directly into the blue lagoon. One of the runners is Heiko who has already taken part in several races in the heat and in the desert. His comment: "I never imagined it would be that hard!" Another runner, Antonio, a wiry Spaniard, comments as a real marathon globetrotter: " Tahiti is even harder than the Hawaii Marathon!"

A mussel as a medal

Running a marathon in the South Seas is a paradox. But the winner, decorated with a medal made from a real mussel and sipping fresh, chilled coconut milk through a straw, does not see it that way. Instead, sitting in the shade of a palm tree, he joins in the discussion about what exact shade of blue the lagoon is now.

"I don't count calories and I certainly love burning them."

Chanamalla Samagond, Inidan short and middle-distance champion

INFORMATION

DATE February

PARTICIPANTS About 150 starters

PACIFIC OCEAN

SOLOMON ISLANDS
PAPUA- NEW GUINEA

Coral Sea   VANUATU

North Fiji Basin   FIJI   **39** •
Tahiti

NEW CALEDONIA

AUSTRALIA

CHARACTER OF THE ROUTE Locals also take part in the lovingly organized marathon weekend but few of them run the actual marathon distance. The turnaround circuit on Moorea is almost completely flat. The heat can sometimes be a problem, especially if there are no clouds, but there are numerous refreshment stations. These offer fresh fruit as well as drinks—and they are probably the most beautiful refreshment stations in the world.

ENTRY FEE From $85 (£60)

THE REGION Tahiti is one of the most distant travel destinations, being 13 hours from New York and 9 hours from Los Angeles. Tahiti is the main island of the Society Islands and Moorea is its "little sister." It is very well developed and offers tourists a wide range of activities, especially water sports such as diving and surfing. The sea is always warm so it is possible to swim at any time of the day or night.

TIP FOR RUNNERS The Pacific is extremely strong so runners must be sure to use a cream with very high sun protection factor. Because of the heat, runners should add about one hour to their average target time.

CONTACT DETAILS
Association Te Moorea Club
Pao Pao, île de Moorea
BP 3385, Temae 98728, Moorea
Polynésie Française
Tel. & Fax: +689/55 08 37 oder +689/56 25 79
Internet: www.mooreamarathon.com

Sahara Marathon

Running tracks in the sand

The Sahara is not listed as one of the most popular travel destinations. Anyone going to the desert either has no choice—or is looking for a challenge. There is no doubt that runners in the Sahara Marathon are in the second category and by participating they are supporting a humanitarian project.

Inhospitable places such as deserts put people off and at the same time they have a special appeal. The Sahara is not a typical stamping ground of runners, much less marathon runners. But it is for this very reason that it attracts an increasing number of runners who want to prove themselves and to show that it is possible, against all reason. People who run in the desert are looking for a unique running experience and that they will find here, but it will be even more intense than expected. The days are hot but the nights are sometimes bitterly cold. The atmosphere and the mood are unique.

But there is something more to the Sahara Marathon: the event is a charity run. Part of the registration fee you pay as a runner is earmarked for UN Refugee Relief projects. These help people who live here near Tindouf, Algeria, not because they chose to but because they have been driven from their original home:

about 170,000 refugees have lived here for over 35 years. "For over ten years the marathon has been drawing attention to the plight of these refugees," Dietmar Kappe of UN Refugee Relief explains. "They were driven from the West Saharan colony and have lived for 35 years in refugee camps where they depend entirely on international help." In the meantime Algeria has offered them a temporary home.

Solidarity in running shoes

The marathon is organized by the Solidarity Committee for the Saharawi people, based in Spain, which also acts as travel agency; there is a special contact person and tour operator for each country. On the one hand, the charity marathon for the Saharawi refugees is a UN-backed project to help their cause. On the other hand, this marathon is also a unique experience, including sharing the living conditions of the Saharawis.

This small field quickly becomes spread out (top). The service points make the run manageable (center). The track is marked with small piles of stones (bottom).

Of course the Sahara Marathon is very different from traditional marathons such as Rome, Paris or Berlin. The marathon runners are housed in the dwellings of the refugee families; this close contact with the families is part of the desert adventure and the marathon experience. Four or five runners are housed in the mud-walled houses or tents where they live with the families and eat together. Thus closeness to the locals develops quite naturally. Temperatures vary from over 68°F (20°C) during the day to about 50°F (10°C) at night.

Running though the dust

The race has its rules and the challenges should not be under-estimated, although they are quite manageable for runners who are well prepared. In recent years the marathon has started in the refugee camp of El Ayoun. The route goes in a North-South direction as far as Smara; it is a point-to-point race. Water points are distributed along the dusty route. No food is provided on the route, but the runners do not complain or miss it. People who enter the desert run know what they are letting themselves in for and they will take their food with them.

How much longer does this marathon take compared to a city marathon? The answer is about 45 minutes: the 2014 winner finished in 2:50:06 hours. The route is marked out with little heaps of stones. In the words of a former participant: "Sand and blue skies extend as far as the eye can see."

"Effort is the one strictly underived and original contribution which we make to the world."

William James, US psychologist and philosopher

INFORMATION

DATE February

PARTICIPANTS About 400 starters

CHARACTER OF THE ROUTE Besides the marathon there are also shorter races. The start of the race is in the refugee camp in the far west of Algeria; the route then takes the runners through some very inhospitable surroundings, but for runners who are looking for something special, while doing something for the refugees, this marathon will be a unique experience.

ENTRY FEE About $1,350 (£800) including flights to and from Madrid. About $210 (£125) of the amount is allocated to humanitarian projects.

THE REGION Tindouf in Algeria. This is not a vacation region and usually the only tourists are just passing through on their way to somehere else. This is why the presence of the runners is so much appreciated as a gesture of solidarity.

TIP FOR RUNNERS The participants come here not only to run but also to support the cause of the marathon and to draw attention to the plight of the Saharawi. It is not just the individual runner but the whole event that carries a message here.

CONTACT DETAILS
Internet: www.saharamarathon.org

Tokyo Marathon

The day we unite

It is the most popular marathon in the world: more runners want to take part in the Tokyo Marathon than in any other marathon, including New York. It was only in 2007 that the Japanese capital finally made up its mind to close off its streets for the marathon. A real success story.

The Tokyo Marathon is one of the world's greatest running events. The organization is perfect and the enthusiasm of the Japanese supporters for the marathon is tremendous.

The Tokyo Marathon was first held in 2007. The fact that it is so recent is hard to believe when you run through the streets of the Japanese capital with its 13 million inhabitants. The Japanese are crazy about marathons, obsessively so! The approval was preceded by a long campaign to persuade the authorities. Anyone who is familiar with Tokyo's traffic can easily imagine the difficulties and challenges facing the urban planners in closing off the city's streets for the marathon, although there had already been a number of elite marathons for smaller groups of top runners. But it was the right thing to do: the marathon is a mass sport and a mass spectacle that is good for the city. And runners are aware of this. Some 30,000 runners take part, although well over 300,000 would like to do so: there are more applications for the Tokyo Marathon than for the New York one!

The world's most popular marathon
Even before 2007 some "marathon activists" were organizing their own Tokyo marathon, running through the streets busy with traffic, stopping at the lights, buying their food in supermarkets along the route—and demonstrating in support of a large-scale marathon.

The marathon started with a bang in 2007. Even the adverse weather conditions of the first year, often repeated subsequently, could not dim the fans' enthusiasm.

Anyone who achieves a top time in the Japanese capital deserve the greatest respect. People who have done so include the Swiss Viktor Röthlin, who set the course record in 2008 and the German Irina Mikitenko in 2013 who ran mostly on her own, battling against a gusty wind and finishing third. Or Claudia Dreher who after her victory in 2008 went into raptures: "The Tokyo Marathon is fantastic experience because running is incredibly popular in Japan. The enthusiasm of the Japanese for the marathon is terrific." Claudia Dreher believes the runners are in a privileged position: "Tokyo is already imposing when you visit the city as a tourist, but as a runner you get a completely different impression of its culture, the people, this lovely, modern mega-city." She also recommends the Tokyo Marathon for amateur runners: "Recognition and respect for achievement are very great in Japan, whether you cross the finish line in first place or last."

Meanwhile the Tokyo Marathon has received international recognition by being accepted as a member of the "Marathon Majors," the association of the big-city marathons of Boston, Chicago, New York, London and Berlin. Tokyo fits in perfectly.

Like in Paris
The runners will form an excellent impression of Tokyo, passing through the typical big-city streets, the harbor area and past various tourist sights lining the route. This starts with the Tokyo Metropolitan Government Building, which has an observation platform for visitors on the 45th floor. There are further attractions along the route such as the Yasakuni Shrine, the Imperial Palace, Shiba Park and the Tokyo Tower. This will look familiar to many: it looks like the Eiffel Tower painted red. It is indeed modeled on the Paris Eiffel Tower but it is a few feet higher, of course.

Tokyo is quite a windy city and the temperatures often drop below 50°F (10°C). But the spectators continue to cheer and encourage the runners tirelessly, enjoying the sight of all runners dressed up in crazy costumes as well as traditional ones: this too is typically Japanese.

»Running a perfect fit for a mindeset like mine. I like being independent and individualistic."

Haruki Murakami, Autor

INFORMATION

DATE End of February

PARTICIPANTS About 35,000 starters

CHARACTER OF THE ROUTE The mostly flat city circuit gives a good impression of the Japanese capital even though only a fraction of the route runs through the city. The Tokyo Marathon is an experience in its own right.

ENTRY FEE About $120 (£70)

THE CITY 13 million of the 126 million inhabitants of Japan live in the Tokyo Metropolis. The city is an important business and commercial center—51 of the world's top 500 companies have their headquarters here. Tourists will manage very well in Tokyo with a little preparation. Everything is punctual and orderly, but at the same time it also hectic with crowds of people everywhere. The visit is well worthwhile and not too expensive when cleverly planned.

TIP FOR RUNNERS Anyone who has already taken part in several marathons will discover new experiences in Japan. The Japanese are marathon-mad and the organization is excellent.

CONTACT DETAILS
Tokyo Marathon Foundation
KNT Tokyo Marathon Entry Desk
Global Business Management Branch
Sumitomo-shoji Kanda-Izumi-choBldg. 12F
1-13 Kanda-Izumi-cho, Chiyoda-ku
Tokyo 101-0024
Japan
Tel.: +81/3/68 91 96 00
Fax: +81/3/68 91 95 99
E-Mail: tm2013@or.knt.co.jp
Internet: www.tokyo42195.org

Antalya Marathon

On the "other" Riviera

The French Rivera may be better known, but the Turkish Riviera has its very special charm—which the runners will discover in Antalya. Also known as "Runtalya," the marathon gives a great impression of this picturesque coastal stretch and it is tempting to combine it with a short break or a longer holiday.

In Turkey running has become an increasingly popular sport. The Antalya Marathon (one of the events of Runtalya) has contributed a lot to this: it reveals the fascinating region around the fifth-largest city in Turkey from a different, sports-orientated point of view. About one-third of the participants come from outside Turkey to take part in the various races, which include the marathon, the half-marathon, the 10K race and the Fun Run.

The fringe events contribute to the appeal of the marathon, such as the very much shorter High Heels Run over 110 yards (100 m), held the day before the main race. All this, combined with the picturesque route and pleasant climate, contribute to a very successful overall package. The almost completely flat route takes the runners through the city, then into the country along the coast road by the Mediterranean with its beautiful views. There is a holiday atmosphere in the air. And this is

the advantage this city has over the other big Turkish marathon, the Istanbul Marathon.

The perfect running climate
Known as "Heaven on earth," Antalya is on the Turkish Riviera, nestling between the sea and the Taurus mountains. Its geographic location to the south of this mountain range 9,842 ft (3,000 m) high—where people ski in winter—gives it an extremely pleasant climate. On clear days you can see the beautiful snow-covered peaks of the mountains that are also now being discovered by mountain bikers and individual cyclists. There is a superb view of the surroundings from the top of the Hidirlik tower, 46 ft (14 m) high. Taller still is the Yivli minaret, the symbol of the town, 125 ft (38 m) high.

The route and the infrastructure are admirable and in view of the pleasant climate near the Mediterranean it is easy to see why this region, steeped

The start of the Antalya Marathon with the snow-capped Taurus Mountains in the background. In the clear air it feels as if you could touch them with yout fingertips (top). The level course means that times can be quick (center and bottom).

in history, has become a tourist magnet, attracting many foreigners as well as Turkish tourists who spend their holidays here in the summer. The recently expanded Antalya airport makes it an easy place to get to.

The marathon is held at the beginning of March, which is still the off-peak season, so the presence of the marathon runners is much appreciated by the locals as well as being enjoyable for them. Also, an increasing number of runners are discovering that the pleasant climate is ideally suited for their spring training.

Relaxation for marathon runners
The organization of the marathon has been highl praised in recent years by the participants. The

marathon organizer is also a tour operator and so looks after the travel arrangements of the many participants who come from abroad. In addition, prices are very reasonable because it is the off-peak season. So the visiting runners are good for the tour operator but the situation also benefits them. It is tempting to add a few days' holiday to relax after the marathon.

Another tip is to treat yourself to a visit to the Turkish Baths, the hammam, including a traditional massage. There is no better way to relax after the marathon.

More and more runners are discovering the Antalya Marathon as a good way to relax and train. It is also an excellent preparation competition for the running season.

"Finishing a marathon is not just an athletic achievement. It is a state of mind."
John Hanc

INFORMATION

DATE Early March

PARTICIPANTS Over 2,000 starters

CHARACTER OF THE ROUTE The route is mostly flat asphalt, a surface that is also suitable for novice marathon runners. The temperatures along the coastal stretch are very pleasant but even in March the strength of the sun should not be underestimated and it is important to use a good sunscreen.

ENTRY FEE From $42 (£25)

THE CITY In recent years Antalya has become a boom town on the Mediterranean with over one million inhabitants. The main reason for this is the growing tourist trade that is now its main source of income. Everything is geared to tourism of all kinds and there is a wide range of cultural and leisure activities available. These include numerous shopping facilities both for designer goods and

examples of local craftsmanship—but you must be prepared to haggle in the markets.

TIP FOR RUNNERS Those who want to run in the resort should mention it to the tour operator, asking for a hotel near the sea promenade where it is possible to run, especially in the morning before it gets too hot.

CONTACT DETAILS
Registration is through a tour operator.

Index

Whether on Tahiti, in the Alps
or in France (from the top),
running has many facets!

Whether alone (top) or in a group (center, bottom), in the cold or in the heat: The Marathon opens the door to experience different worlds.

Responsabile editoriale: Beate Dreher
Redazione: Daniela Hansjakob, München
Progetto grafico: graphitecture book
& edition
Copertina: Karin Vollmer, kv@designtotal.eu
Cartografia: Astrid Fischer-Leitl, München

All the facts in this book have been carefully researched and updated as well as being proofread by the publisher. However, no liability can assumed for the accuracy of the content.

Cover:
Top: Runners in the Berlin Marathon (picture alliance/Camera4)
Bottom: Runners in the Sydney Marathon on the world-famous Sydney Harbour Bridge (picture-alliance/dpa/dpaweb)

Back cover: Runners in the Paris Marathon (left, E. Vargiolu); enthusiastic spectators at the New York Marathon (right, Norbert Wilhelmi)

The author

Urs Weber has been working as an editor at *Runner's World*, the biggest specialist running magazine, for over ten years, thus combining his hobby and his work, because he has been an enthusiastic runner since boyhood. He has taken part in marathons for over twenty-five years, at least once a year but usually several times a year. Besides the big cities, he also tries to choose marathons in places where he has never been such as the Himalayas, the South Seas or the Arctic Circle. There he takes part as a runner taking photographs or as a photographer who is running. As a result he has taken part in numerous marathons throughout the world, both as a journalist and runner.

Photograph credits

All photographs inside the book are from Norbert Wilhelmi, except:
picture alliance/Camera4, pp. 6/7; Urs Weber, p. 8 c./b.; pp. 9 t., 28, 29, 30, 31, 32, 33, 34; picture alliance/augenklick, p. 10 t.; picture-alliance/dpa, p. 11 t.; picture alliance/ZB, pp. 12, 22, 23, 24; Urs Weber, pp. 14 t./c., 15 b., 16 t./b., 17, 38 b., 46 t., 50 b., 58, 59, 70 t., 92, 93, 94, 95, 116, 130, 131, 132, 133, 135, 136 t./re., 138 c., 151, 154, 155, 162 t./b., 163 t./c.; Victah Sailer, pp. 14 b., 15 t., 16 c., 36 t./b., 37, 38 t., 39, 96, 97, 98, 99, 106, 107, 108, 109, 110, 111, 142/143, 144, 145, 158, 159; Wildfrontiers, p. 20; laufreisen.de/ Nils Krekenbaum, p. 21 t.; picture-alliance/ dpa, pp. 22 c./b., 24 b./re., 25, 60 t./c./b., 57, 74 t./c., 78 t., 100 c., 124 c. EVA/ Ap./E. Vargiolu, pp. 26, 27; shutterstock, pp. 38 c. 47, 50 t./c., 51, 109 b., 110 b., 118, 119; picture alliance/AP Images, pp. 36 c. 139 t., 140 b.; picture alliance/ Arco Images GmbH, p. 44; fotolia, p. 45; Marianne Mangold, p. 48 t.; MarathonFoto, p. 48 c.; Reg Regalado, pp. 48 b., 50 re.; Douglas Steakley, p. 49 t.; swiss-image.ch, pp. 56/57, 80, 81, 82, 83, 90/91, 162 c.; Martin Ekequist, pp. 64 t., 65 b., 66 re.; RF = Rickard Forsberg, pp. 64 c./b., 65 t., 66 t./b., 67; Salomon, p. 69; Merell, pp. 69, 70 b., 71, 73, 153; picture alliance/landov, pp. 74 b., 138 c. 140 c.; picture alliance/Klaus Nowottnick, p. 75; Adventure Marathon, pp. 76, 77; Daryan Dornelles/Runner's World Brazil, p. 78 b.; picture alliance/Chris Wallberg, p. 79; Julbo, p. 84; Eric Vargiolu, p. 85; Petri Krook, pp. 88, 89; Craig Golding, p. 100 t./b.; picture-alliance/Actionplus, p. 101; picture alliance/Sueddeutsche Zeitung Photo, pp. 113 b.,115; Ed Turk fotografie, pp. 124 t./b., 125; Fotos Grönland Tourism, pp. 134, 136 c./b., 137; picture alliance/ AA, p. 141; Standard Chartered Marathon Singapore, pp. 148, 149; Polar, p. 152; Wolfgang Hofmann, p. 156 t./b.; Dietmar Kappe, pp. 156 c., 157; H. Dullink, p. 163 b., Robert Grischek, p. 168 (Portrait Urs Weber)

t. = top, c. = center, b. = bottom

© 2014 Bruckmann Verlag GmbH, München

WS White Star Publishers® is a registered trademark property of
De Agostini Libri S.p.A..

© 2014 De Agostini Libri S.p.A.
Via G. da Verrazano, 15
28100 Novara, Italy
www.whitestar.it - www.deagostini.it

Translation and Editing:
Rosetta Translations SARL

ISBN 978-88-544-0892-0
1 2 3 4 5 6   18 17 16 15 14

Printed in China

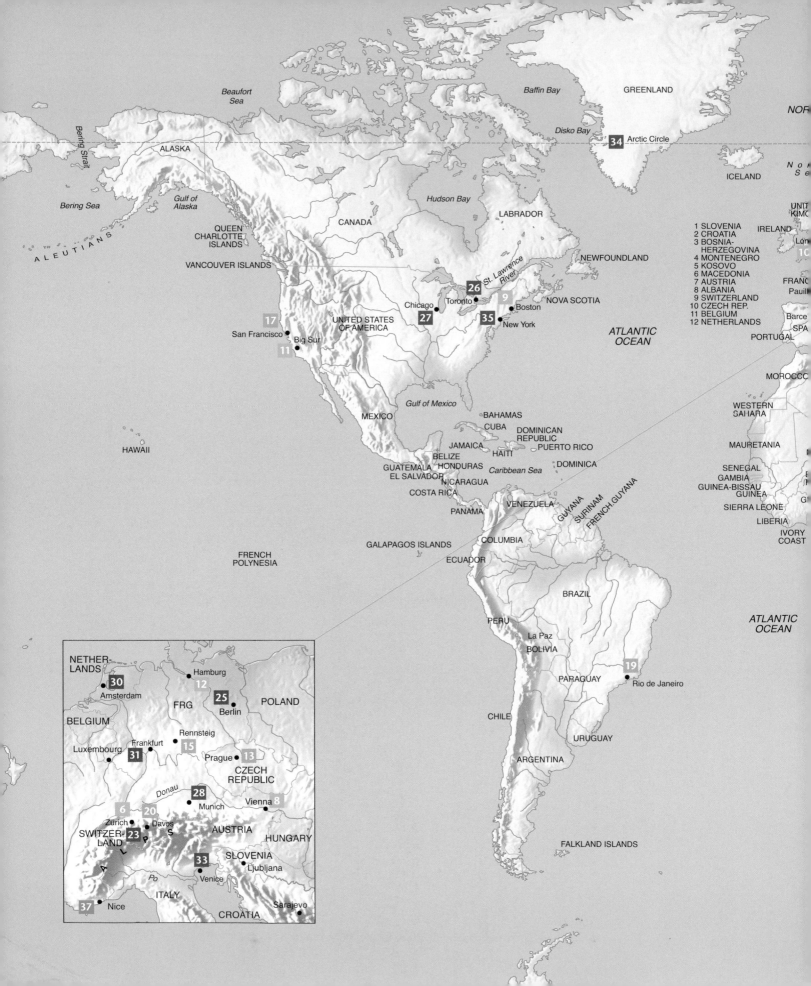

NOR

GREENLAND

Baffin Bay

Beaufort
Sea

Bering Strait

Disko Bay
34 Arctic Circle

ICELAND

N O
S e

ALASKA

Bering Sea

Gulf of
Alaska

A L E U T I A N S

CANADA

HUDSON BAY

LABRADOR

NEWFOUNDLAND

QUEEN
CHARLOTTE
ISLANDS

VANCOUVER ISLANDS

St. Lawrence
River

NOVA SCOTIA

26
Toronto
Chicago
27
9
Boston
35
New York

17
San Francisco
Big Sur
11

UNITED STATES
OF AMERICA

ATLANTIC
OCEAN

Gulf of Mexico

MEXICO

BAHAMAS
CUBA
DOMINICAN
REPUBLIC
JAMAICA   PUERTO RICO
HAITI
BELIZE
GUATEMALA HONDURAS   DOMINICA
EL SALVADOR   Caribbean Sea
NICARAGUA
COSTA RICA
PANAMA   VENEZUELA

UNIT
KIM
IRELAND
Lo

1 SLOVENIA
2 CROATIA
3 BOSNIA-
   HERZEGOVINA
4 MONTENEGRO
5 KOSOVO
6 MACEDONIA
7 AUSTRIA
8 ALBANIA
9 SWITZERLAND
10 CZECH REP.
11 BELGIUM
12 NETHERLANDS

FRANC
Pauil

Barce
SPA

PORTUGAL

MOROCCO

WESTERN
SAHARA

MAURETANIA

SENEGAL
GAMBIA
GUINEA-BISSAU
   GUINEA

SIERRA LEONE

LIBERIA

IVORY
COAST

HAWAII

FRENCH
POLYNESIA

GALAPAGOS ISLANDS

GUYANA
SURINAM
FRENCH.GUYANA

COLUMBIA

ECUADOR

PERU

BRAZIL

ATLANTIC
OCEAN

La Paz
BOLIVIA

19
Rio de Janeiro

PARAGUAY

CHILE

URUGUAY

ARGENTINA

FALKLAND ISLANDS

NETHER-
LANDS
30
Amsterdam

BELGIUM

Luxembourg
31

Hamburg
12
FRG
25
Berlin

POLAND

Rennsteig
Frankfurt
15
Prague
13
CZECH
REPUBLIC

Donau
28
Munich
Vienna
8

6 **20**
Zürich Davos
SWITZER-   S
LAND **23**
A
L
P
S
AUSTRIA

HUNGARY

SLOVENIA
Ljubljana
33
Venice

37 Nice

Po

ITALY

CROATIA

Sarajevo

North Pole 7

ARCTIC OCEAN

SPITZBERGEN

NEW SIBERIAN
ISLANDS

Laptev Sea

Barents Sea

Kara Sea

North Cape

KOLA
PENINSULA

Bering Sea

NORWAY

SWEDEN

FINLAND

Helsinki 21

*Sea of
Okhotsk*

KAMTSCHATKA

Stockholm

16

ESTONIA

RUSSIA

LATVIA

Baltic Sea

DENMARK
LITHUANIA

KALININGRAD
OBLAST

FRG

POLAND

BELARUS

2

10

SLOVAKIA

UKRAINE

KAZAKHSTAN

9

7

HUNGARY

MOLDAVIA

Caspian Sea

1

2

ROMANIA

*Aral
Sea*

MONGOLIA

8

SERBIA

UZBEKHISTAN

4

5

BULGARIA

*Black
Sea*

GEORGIA

KIRGHISTAN

NORTH
KOREA

*Sea of
Japan*

1

Rome

8

6

ARMENIA

AZERBAIJAN

TAJIKISTAN

CHINA

Great Wall 14

29

ITALY

GREECE

36

TURKEY

TURKMENISTAN

Osaka JAPAN

SOUTH
KOREA

32

Tokyo

Athens

Antalya 42

Aegean

SYRIA

IRAQ

IRAN

AFGHANISTAN

Himalayas

41

Corsica

*Mediterranean
Sea*

LEBANON
ISRAEL

JORDAN

PAKISTAN

BHUTAN

*South China
Sea*

TUNISIA

NEPAL

LIBYA

EGYPT

SAUDI
ARABIA

QATAR

Red Sea

UNITED
ARAB.
EMIRATES

OMAN

INDIA

BANGLADESH

Mekong

BURMA

LAOS

HONG KONG

TAIWAN

PACIFIC
OCEAN

NIGER

CHAD

SUDAN

ERITREA

YEMEN

VIETNAM

*Gulf of
Bengal*

THAILAND

NIGERIA

CENTRAL
AFRICAN
REPUBLIC

SOUTH
SUDAN

ETHIOPIA

SRI
LANKA

CAMBODIA

PHILIPPINES

CAMEROON

EQUATORIAL
GUINEA

UGANDA

KENYA

SOMALIA

GABON

CONGO

DR CONGO

RUANDA
BURUNDI

3

Kilimanjaro

MALAYSIA

BRUNEI

38

Singapore

Big Five

18

SEYCHELLES

INDONESIA

PAPUA-
NEW GUINEA

SOLOMON
ISLANDS

TANZANIA

BALI

ANGOLA

ZAMBIA

MALAWI

*INDIAN
OCEAN*

NAMIBIA

BOTSWANA

ZIMBABWE

MOZAMBIQUE

ST-MARIE

MAURITIUS

RÉUNION

Coral Sea

VANUATU

FIJI 39

*North Fiji
Basin*

Tahiti

AUSTRALIA

NEW CALEDONIA

SWAZILAND

MADAGASCAR

LESOTHO

4

SOUTH
AFRICA

Sydney

Cape Town

24

Tasman Sea

North Island

NEW ZEALAND

South Island

0   N   1000 km

ANTARCTICA

29.95   8/3/15.